CONTEMPORARY FRENCH WOMEN POETS:
A BILINGUAL CRITICAL ANTHOLOGY

Edited and Translated by

Carl Hermey

PERIVALE PRESS

D1570233

© 1977 by Perivale Press
© 1975 on critical essays and English
translations by Carl William Hermey
Library of Congress Catalog Number 76-3065
International Standard Book Number 0-912288-08-6
Typesetting and design by Biographics
Printing by KNI, Inc.

Published 1977 by
　　　　　PERIVALE PRESS
　　　　　13830 Erwin Street
　　　　　Van Nuys, California 91401

Second printing revised 1978
Distributed by:
　　　　　SPECTRUM PRODUCTIONS
　　　　　979 Casiano Road
　　　　　Los Angeles, California 90049

ACKNOWLEDGEMENT

In putting this book together I felt privileged to be guided by a number of people. At the top of the list is Rainer Schulte of the University of Texas at Dallas. Without his guidance and encouragement the book could never have been written. My essays and translations improved under the watchful eye of Marilyn Gaddis Rose of the State University of New York at Binghamton; to her I am most thankful. Thanks, too, to Jonathan Chaves, Eliane Jasenas, Gayle Whittier and Sandra Smith, all of whom gave the typescript a careful reading and provided valuable suggestions.

INTRODUCTION

Six Contemporary French Poets:
Mirrors of the Mind

This bilingual anthology of contemporary French women poets grew out of my long-time interest in the poetry being written today in Europe and the Americas, and, in particular, the poetry written by French-speaking writers. In my research over the past two years I have noticed that very few women poets from France have received the critical attention which I believe they deserve both in their own countries and this country. In the major bilingual editions of contemporary French verse which have been published in the last decade, only three women are represented, compared with over 80 men.[1] I believe that many good women poets on the contemporary international scene have suffered neglect as a result of their not being represented in the various anthologies, literary histories and critical works which have appeared. With the present anthology, I hope to expand the audience of six of the major women poets writing in French today, thereby encouraging a recognition of their artistic achievements and initiating a critical discussion of their poetry.

These six poets were not chosen just because they are women or because their work embodies a poetic vision which is characteristically feminine. They were chosen because they have written stimulating and imaginative poetry within the important trends of modern French poetry and because they are helping to shape a contemporary poetic vision which goes beyond national and linguistic boundaries.

Poetry which claims to belong to the modern tradition, a movement whose roots extend as far back as Nerval and Baudelaire, is characterized by a non-descriptive mode of expression. In the same way that the Impressionist painters were no longer content to render a copy of the world around them, the modern poet no longer uses words to reproduce a replica of what he experiences. Rather, he imposes his inner vision on the reality around him, thereby bringing about a transformation of the objects he sees. For the reader of modern poetry, then, a more important question than "what does the poem mean?" is "How does the poet see?" Since the poet's inner vision usually focuses on the most elemental impressions from the outside world — light, trees, stones, sun, stars, earth, darkness — he makes the raw materials of his poetic transformations accessible to everyone, and he no

[1] See bibliography, p. 206

i

longer needs to depend on established social, cultural or mythical subjects to frame his vision. By focusing on material immediately accessible to everyone, the poets in this anthology eliminate the need for the reader to situate himself in a given sociological, political or mythical milieu. Thérèse Plantier speaks of such elemental things as water, darkness and sky; Andrée Chedid speaks of fire, earth and chasms; Annie Salager speaks of the furnishings of a room, and then distills these objects into their essence; Marie Françoise Prager speaks of tombs, birds and monsters; Yvonne Caroutch, of stars, rock, wind and silence; and Denise Grappe, of knives, wounds and labyrinths.

The way each individual poet treats these subjects, moreover, gives us a glimpse of the structure of each poet's vision. Plantier wants to plunge into water amidst darkness and turn her back on the sky. Chedid plunges into chasms in order to enkindle her fires. Salager's imagination transforms the furnishings of her room into a series of shapes and textures, and thereby changes her world. Prager willingly enters tombs only to be transformed into birds which defy death. Caroutch's stars are rosy-cheeked; wind tattoos the rock; and silence pricks her fingers. In Grappe, labyrinths uncoil in an instant, and a sacramental offering is drunk from an open wound.

To the extent to which modern poetry reflects the inner dynamics of the human mind, it becomes a poetry of image and metaphor, and it is through the special logic of association that the poet's vision, his transformation of reality, is communicated to us. Further, it is through the constant shifting of these images and associations that the poet reveals the movements of his mind. For example, the following poem taken from Plantier's latest volume, **Jusqu'à ce que l'enfer gèle** ("Till Hell Freezes Over"), moves from an image that is purely photographic in the first line through a series of images that become increasingly more conceptual. They move out of the sensual plane of perception and enter a realm where they can only be conceived within the mind:

> Water in the fields
> rain in the water
> my tears in the rain
> your body in my teardrops
> oblivion in your body
> spaces spaces

> *De l'eau dans les champs*
> *de la pluie dans l'eau*

mes pleurs dans la pluie
ton corps dans mes larmes
l'oubli dans ton corps
l'espace l'espace
(p.17)

Moreover, as the poem shifts from one image to the next, each link in the interlocking chain becomes more closely associated with some human quality or attribute. Water contains rain, which contains tears, which in turn contain a body, which finally contains oblivion. The process of going from "water in the fields" to "oblivion in your body" involves what one might call the expansion of conceptual space. The spaces the poet creates by expanding from horizontal into vertical planes of perception (This space is enunciated in the final line of the poem) is where the aesthetic impact of the poem occurs. It is within these spaces that the poet transforms reality.

The poet achieves this transformation by enabling the reader to experience new perceptions through the words of his poem. I purposely say **"through** the word" rather than "**in** the word," because the poetry which the reader experiences lies in the space between the words which take the reader beyond the usual referents of the word, while keeping him, nonetheless, under the poet's control.

The problem of the poet is to find suitable language to represent his own special perception of the world, a perception that need not necessarily be based on common-sense cause and effect. Whatever final form his language takes, it will reflect his own personal view of both himself and the reality around him. This view is then self-contained in the poem and does not rely on any supportive system of knowledge outside the poem to give it meaning. The end result is a highly personalized poetic vision which reflects the inner dynamics of a single individual, a vision which can be communicated to audiences beyond national boundaries.

Each of the six poets of this anthology creates her own personalized poetic universe through her own characteristic movement of words and images. And to catch a glimpse of what is meant by this movement, one might mention the startling juxtaposition of images, the sudden jolts, and the halting irregular rhythms in the poetry of Thérèse Plantier; the fervent lyricism and brilliant clarity in the lines of Andrée Chedid; the smooth melodious music of Annie Salager that accompanies her alternating shifts between the real world and fantasy. One can also mention the claustrophobic world of Marie-Françoise Prager expanded by strange and fantasmagoric dream states, the wild descriptive quality of Yvonne Caroutch's lines as she gives free reign to her imagination, and finally the suffering and frustration that becomes concretized in the dense poems of Denise Grappe.

The final stage in the whole process of poetic communication is when the reader joins the poet in his movement. This is not easily accomplished because the language of the poem, since it reflects the mind, need not be logical, and because words, ultimately, are only signs which may render imperfectly a mental state which is, at the outset, foreign to the reader. The reader is therefore required to make a tremendous effort to understand the poem. This effort, however, is rewarded by a deep appreciation of the poem, an appreciation rendered more intense by the sense that the reader has actually created a new psychic experience and invented a new part of himself. The reading of the poem is thereby the linguistic act of re-creation of oneself, the poem, and the poet.

TRANSLATION PROBLEMS

The primary task of the translator is to visualize what is going on beyond or below the words of the poem. In order to visualize, the translator reconstructs the process that went on in the poet's mind and which ultimately led the poet to represent that process with a particular set of words.

It is not my intention to theorize about the translation of poetry or to contribute to the large number of theoretical pronouncements which have already been made on the subject. I have listed several of these in the bibliography. But I would like to emphasize my general belief that the translator should be as faithful as possible to the original. This involves not only the accurate transformation of the poem's language into English but also making sure that the magical quality of the language, that which makes it poetry, does not get lost in the transferral. Since much of modern poetry derives its power from the ambiguity of words, it is often impossible to find English cognates which accurately reproduce these powers of multiple suggestion. Thus it is often necessary to search around in what might be called the "magnetic field" of the word for the best solution. The following discussion of some of the specific problems I have encountered in these translations will illustrate what I mean.

Very often these problems consist of words with multiple meanings in French. Sometimes pure chance enables the translator to find an English word with the same meaning, but more often than not, in a case like this one must decide which meaning the original word visualized. In the following lines from Thérèse Plantier,

> *il y a un arbre dans les barques*
> *aux pontons du ciel amarrées.*

the word **"ponton"** can mean either "pontoon," "prison ship," "hulk," "pontoon bridge" or "landing." Since the poem is about eternity being within a tree rather than within the sky, and since ships are often associated with people in Plantier, it seemed to me that "prison ships" would be a good solution:

> there is a tree in the ships
> moored to the prison ships of the sky.

But there were obvious problems because of literalness and, because of the confusing repetition of "ships". I then began to try other alternatives. "Pontoons" had the wrong connotation in English; "hulk" was too vague. "Pontoon bridge" added a meaning inconsistent with Plantier's overall view—bridges connecting man with the sky. "Landings" certainly fit in rhythmically with the line and was logical: "moored to the landings of the sky." But because of the very appropriateness of "landings" to "moored" the line lacked intensity. I finally settled on simply "prisons," first, because the meaning fits in with Plantier's view of things—we are trapped in the heavens—and because "prisons of the sky" has the same visual impact as any other dark, massive object floating in mid-air. Final version:

> in the boats moored to the prisons of the
> sky there is a tree.

An instance where I was able to preserve a multiple meaning occurs in Salager's poem "A Certain Hatred of Poetry." Here she describes the poetic imagination as

> *Cailloux, ô mes chemins, trames inachevées*

"Trame" in the above context means either a piece of "woven fabric" or a "thread" or "intrigue" of a story. I was able to catch both senses by substituting for the adjective **"inachevées"** the word "unwoven" which can refer to an unfinished story thread or an incompleted piece of weaving. **"Chemins"** presented no problem. Final solution:

> Pebbles, O my roads of unwoven intrigues

Sometimes a passage will only have meaning if placed into a certain cultural context; then the translator must find an appropriate equivalent which has meaning for the English-speaking reader. The following lines which occur in a poem about bad poets by Plantier, originally puzzled me:

> *ils se passent l'anneau violet*
> *font courir le furet*
> *il court il court*

Passing a purple ring and making a ferret run made no sense to me on any level in the poem. A native speaker then informed me that this is a school children's game where a ring is passed from child to child in a circle, to the accompaniment of a little song: *"il court il court, le furet . . . "* In a letter which Plantier later wrote to me mentioning some examples of what she considered bad poetry, she used another children's song, with which I was familiar, to describe the infantile efforts of certain poets. All this convinced me that I should try to find an equivalent English nursery rhyme that would also capture the frivolous going-around-in-circles of Plantier's rhymesters. I think this catches it:

They fill their pockets full of posey
make their rings around the rosey.

Often it is necessary to change the syntax of a whole stanza in order to preserve the flow of the original in English. The opening lines of Salager's piece **Night of the Poem, Perfect Love** will illustrate the necessity of syntactical rearrangement:

La nuit si lente à accomplir ses rites
il me semble
— mais est-ce possible —
proche très proche s'agenouille.

A word-for-word rendering would give us the following:

The night so slow to accomplish its rite
it seems to me
— but is it possible —
close so close kneels down

There are two typically French constructions in this passage which simply cannot be rendered directly into English without sounding awkward or pedestrian: the long adjectival phrase *"si lente à accomplir ses rites"* modifying *"la nuit,"* and the inverted verb and adverb *"proche très proche s'agenouille."* I solved this problem by beginning the sentence with "it seems" and then changing the long adjectival phrase into a verb. The final version reads much simpler and certainly flows more easily than the literal rendering:

It seems
— but can it be —
that night kneels down close by
and celebrates its slow ritual.

A dangerous tendency in translation is to use the word which is the most obvious equivalent in the target language. These literal renderings often destroy the visual impact that the image has in the original, and consequently it is necessary to use a word with a slightly different meaning in the target language in order to produce an accurate visualization. For example, in one of Chedid's poems, the word sometimes (literally) "shoves the grills of language" *("bouscule les grilles du langage")*. By searching through the various associations of the verb *"bousculer"* and the noun *"grille,"* I came up with the following solution:

Sometimes the word
rattles the cages of language

which I think is a more accurate visualization of what is happening in that line. The same process occurs in the translation of these lines from Caroutch:

> ... *les autres qui traversent*
> *le lacis indéchiffré*
> *de nos signes*

The English cognate for **"signe,"** "sign," does not carry the same association as the original, and also has a very concrete secondary meaning which might cause the reader to think of a signboard. The following solution, though not accurate in a literal sense, does provide clearer visualization of the line:

> ... The others who cross
> the undeciphered web
> of our gestures.

One final observation I should like to make concerns the very special intimacy with the poem which one gains by translating it into one's native tongue. Translation requires one not only to enter the world of the poet, but also to recreate his world. Unlike those critics who speak **about** the poem or the poet, the translator speaks from a unique position **within** the voice of the poet, a voice which he must echo in another language.

ANDREE CHEDID

ANDREE CHEDID:
THE SEARCH FOR THE PRIVILEGED MOMENT

For Andrée Chedid, poetry is a never-ending quest for life's hidden essence, the stable truth which outlives the ephemeral shadows of the real world. Chedid immediately takes the reader into her personal poetic quest. This quest is a mosaic of intense, often violent, metaphorical juxtapositions which do not operate on a single perceptual plane. Because of this intensity, the reader is forced to participate actively in the poem, and to see the world through the eye of the poet:

> Poetry needs only us to come to life.
> *La poésie n'attend que nous pour être.*
>
> **(Visage premier,** back cover)

The object of Chedid's quest is variously identified as "Life," "the source" (which in French has the added meaning of well-spring), and "the primal face." It is significant that Chedid uses a variety of terms to name her inquiry of the philosophical nature of truth. The multiplicity of terms used to describe this ideal not only reflects the evasiveness of "truth," its refusal to be pinned down and codified, but also the desire of the poet to expand her idiom, to make it more communicable to a variety of readers who themselves bring differing visions and sensibilities to the poem. In the poem entitled **Visage premier**("The Primal Face"), Chedid shows us that this primal face, although it lives within us, is elusive and not easily grasped:

> When man has expanded himself
> to the limits of all his lives
> You'll disappear over the crest
> of the highest metamorphosis.
>
> *Quand l'homme se sera étiré*
> *jusqu'aux limites de toutes ses vies*
> *Tu disparaîtras sur la crête*
> *de l'extrême métamorphose.*
>
> **(Visage premier,** p. 9)

It becomes apparent that Chedid sees the world in a state of continuous metamorphosis. Whatever her imagination touches becomes transformed through her most personal innovative perception. She succeeds in establishing a relationship with objects around her that gives the reader the impression that he is looking at these objects for the first time. Many of Chedid's poems deal with those special, privileged moments when we break the confines of space and time and catch a glimpse of the primal face. These instants do not come often or easily, as the poem **Passage to the Source** (p. 13) illustrates. It is only after time lets us pass freely through its difficult path, only after a slow growth to the edge of the horizon, that we can utter words that name the source. And this, only after we have been made "more profound by an omen / more grave by an ordeal" ("*plus profonds d'un présage / plus graves d'une épreuve*").

The object of Chedid's search, whether it is called "source," "face," or "Life," is almost invariably associated with images of fire and light:

> That the spring may flow
> That life may live
> The fire must burn.
>
> *Il nous faut l'incendie*
> *Pour que s'amorce la source*
> *Pour que vive la vie.*
>
> **(Visage premier, p. 41)**

It is within this fire that she recognizes the primal face:

> But I know
> Your face
> in the forge of your fire.
>
> *Mais je te sais*
> *De face*
> *Dans la forge de ton feu.*
>
> **(Visage premier, p. 12)**

Consistently, the spark that enkindles this fire is poetry itself:

> Poetry
> you lead us
> to the substance of the world . . .
> You search the empty spaces
> You encircle the fire
>
> *Poésie*
> *Tu nous mène*
> *vers la substance du monde . . .*
> *Questionnant la clairière*
> *Cernant tout le brasier.*
>
> **(Visage premier, p. 54)**

For Chedid, the process of poetic communication is an act of self-liberation which, at once, breaks her bonds and makes her one with the fire:

> ... with a sign
> I break my bonds
> My poem soars
> Lightning captures me.

> ... *d'un signe*
> *Je me délie*
> *Le chant plane*
> *L'éclair me tient.*

(Visage premier, p. 17)

The search for these privileged moments when the poet becomes one with the fire carries her not only upward to the heavens, but also downward into the abyss. Unlike Plantier, who constantly seeks out darkness, and for whom the abyss is always shrouded in shadow, Chedid always moves toward light and can find it even in the dark shadows of the underworld: "I plunge into chasms / to enkindle the instant" (*"Je plonge dans les gouffres / pour embraser l'instant"*).

Closely connected with the image of fire is that of fusion. Fusion is implicit in her numerous references to becoming one with the fire. This fusion, this integration, is at the very heart of Chedid's poetic, for it is through the union of the self with the outside world, or, to put it another way, the intersection of the poet with the object of her vision, that "Life" is created:

> Sometimes I become
> what I have named
> Then
>
> LIFE!
>
> Sometimes

> *Parfois je deviens*
> *ce que j'ai nommé*
> *Alors*
>
> *LA VIE!*
>
> *Parfois*

(Contre-chant, p. 28)

It is by seeing the world around her through another eye, what she calls *"l'autre regard,"* that the poet attains this special kind of intimacy with her world. Throughout Chedid's poetry we see a concern for "sharing words." That is, the poet tries to make the word reflect not only a part of the reality around her, but also the particular way in which the poet receives and interprets

4

that reality. This concern may be illustrated by the poem "Step I" (p. 29). Here the poet tries to join the earth to her earth. What she is attempting to do is to reconcile the difference between the real world and the poet's conception of it by interposing a medium of communication between them—the word. This poem records the process of joining "words to the cunning of silence," and "open sea to a sail-draped hymn." In each of the above three lines a part of the poetic consciousness—"my earth," "words," "sail-draped hymn"—is fused to a corresponding but sometimes antagonistic reality outside the poet—"the earth," "the cunning of silence," "open sea." To accomplish this difficult fusion, it is necessary to bend words to the sharing point. Throughout Chedid's poetry we find images of bridges and arches which represent the process of the word becoming more than just a word, becoming a powerful fusing force which is capable of uniting two separate consciousnesses: "words extend bridges" *("les mots lancent des passerelles")*. In the poem, **Amarres, notre liberté,** (p. 57) ("Chains, Our Freedom"), words are characterized as bonds which, paradoxically, create our freedom. When days "bog down" and "block our avenues," when they "scatter tomorrow with rocks," and "grow stiff upon our meadows," it is then that we must "draw life from a face" and remember the arches we share." The bond which words create between ourselves and the world destroys the chains that bind us to space and time: "our words engulf the shadowed doors / our bonds set freedom free."

One must recognize, though, that Chedid's bridges are not built easily. For often our own voices prevent words from communicating. Even though words are stronger than voices,

> Words, I know you well
> So patiently constructed
> With arches
> More steadfast than our voices

> *Je te connais, Parole*
> *Si patiemment construite,*
> *Avec tes arceaux*
> *Plus tenaces que nos voix.*
> **(Contre-chant, p. 56)**

sometimes they cannot bridge the deep chasms that separate them:

> From one voice to another
> the bridges resist
>
> *D'une voix à l'autre*
> *les passerelles résistent*
> **(Visage premier, p. 18)**

It is through words, then, and through their ability to arch over and bridge the gap between the self and the world (or the self and other selves) that life is created.

Earlier it was demonstrated how Chedid's concept of the primal face is closely associated with fire and light. In close harmony with this image is the idea that arches or bridges can destroy darkness and shadow:

> With the arch of words . . .
> You will break out of darkness
> You will see!
>
> *Avec l'arc des mots . . .*
> *Tu franchiras les ténèbres*
> *Tu verras!*
> **(Contre-chant, p. 26)**

In fact, a consistent pattern throughout Chedid's poetry is the conquest of light over darkness, and the invasion and destruction of darkness by bridges and arches:

> When dawn embraces the city
> The future erects arches
> And memory pulls embers from the shadow
>
> *Quand l'aube s'éprend de la ville*
> *L'avenir élève ses arches*
> *La mémoire tire braises de l'ombre*
> **(Visage premier, p. 24)**

The power of the word itself is an important theme with Chedid and, like the conflict of light and darkness, we see a conflict also of word and silence: "certain words shatter all the silence we must live" *("certaines paroles bouleversent tout le silence à vivre")*. The poem **The Surging Word** (p. 31) is a perfect illustration of its magical powers. Here the word breaks the confines of language and the artificial strictures that language imposes on us. It "rattles the cages of language," it "escapes the rule of words." It is the word which, once broken free from the confines of language, leads us to the privileged instant: "sometimes the word captures an instant from the flow of time" *("parfois le mot emporte et chevauche ma durée").* At the point where the poet becomes one with her word, life is created.

It is important to remember that Chedid's poetry is not one prolonged ecstatic union with the word. Her instants do not come often, nor are they long: "the instant is so brief that unveils the fusion" *("l'instant est si bref qui dévoile l'accord").* As in the poem cited above, it is only "sometimes" that the word exerts its power. The instant plants its seed in us, but often we will not permit it to grow:

> The instant casts a seed
> But silently our earth rejects it
> Never naming the flower.
>
> *L'instant sème.*
> *Mais nos terres l'éconduisent*
> *Sans nommer sa fleur.*
>
> **(Contre-chant, p. 59)**

Often, shadows dominate the light: "what else can we do but tend our shadows" *("que faisons-nous d'autre / que jardiner nos ombres")* and, "until the ultimate transparence," shadows will "deceive our lives."

Chedid's poetry is not an endless celebration of life, for death is always present, often associated with silence. In the poem **Silence à vivre** ("Silence to Live"), she talks of how death is constantly with us:

> Certain tombs do not yellow with age
> Certain deaths multiply our anguish
> Certain departures bring on new suffering.
>
> *Certaines tombes ne jaunissent pas*
> *Certaines fins multiplient le vertige . . .*
> *Certains départs s'adossent à la fraîche souffrance.*
>
> **(Visage premier, p. 22)**

Death is important for Chedid, because it intensifies life, because faced with death, we come together.

> It is our only certainty, the seal of our
> common destiny. The thought of death
> unites us all. It waits for us. We will all go
> to meet it.
>
> *C'est notre seule certitude, le sceau de*
> *notre destiné commune. L'idée de la mort*

> *nous réunit tous. Elle nous attend. Nous*
> *allons tous la rejoindre.* [1]

Death is the "companion who sets the instant in motion" *("compagne, qui retimbre la durée").* It is the spark of creativity: "we can only build when death is close by" *("nous ne pourrons bâtir qu'adossés à la mort").*

Chedid's poetry does not give us any simple answers to the human condition. Her poems record more of a process, a movement towards a final goal, more than an arrival there. As was said earlier, her poetry is a never-ending quest. In this context, the idea of metamorphosis is illuminating. When we have extended ourselves to the limit of our life, the primal face still eludes us "over the crest of the highest metamorphosis" *("sur la crête de l'ultime métamorphose").* But the voyage is more fulfilling and enriching than any final resting place. For Chedid, it is better that we actually fall short of our goal, that we be eternal "passengers of the metamorphosis" *("passagers de la métamorphose").*

[1] Magazine Littéraire, 31 (1969), p. 42.

ANDREE CHEDID

Andrée Chedid was born in Cairo but has lived in Paris since 1946. She is perhaps the most well known French woman poet writing today. In addition to poetry she has also published short stories, novels, and, most recently, plays. Many of her prose and theatrical works deal with Egyptian themes. Most of her early volumes of poems (beginning in 1949) were published by Guy-Lévis-Mano, and were collected in 1965 under the title **Double-Pays.** She was awarded the Louise Labé prize in 1966. Her published works include the following volumes of poetry:

Textes pour une figure (Pré aux Clercs, 1949)
Textes pour un poème (G.L.M., 1950)
Textes pour le vivant (G.L.M., 1953)
Textes pour la terre aimée (G.L.M., 1955)
Terre regardée (G.L.M., 1957)
Seul, le visage (G.L.M., 1960)
Lubies (G.L.M., 1962)
Double-Pays (G.L.M., 1965)
Contre-Chant (Flammarion, 1968)
Visage premief (Flammarion, 1972)
La Fraternité de la parole (Flammarion, 1976)

VISAGE PREMIER

Tu présides à toute naissance
A ton front se nouent
l'ancêtre et le futur

Visage très stable
pierre de nos fragments
Tu demeures en chacune de nos faces

Nos plaies ne viendront jamais à bout
de ta fraîcheur

Angle de tous les possibles
Source jamais tarie
tu engrènes l'aventure singulière
Puis   la résorbe au loin

Quand l'homme se sera étiré
jusqu'aux limites de toutes ses vies

Tu disparaîtras sur la crête
de l'extrême métamorphose.

Visage premier, p. 9

THE PRIMAL FACE

You preside every birth
Forefather and future unite
at your brow

Most stable face
Rock of our fragments
You remain in each of our faces

Our wounds will never vanquish
your innocence

Crossroads of all possibilities
Ever-flowing spring
you nourish the uncommon adventure
Then recapture it in the distance

When man has extended himself
to the limits of all his lives

You'll disappear over the crest
of the highest metamorphosis.

PASSAGE DE LA SOURCE

Quand les fourrés du temps
nous cèdent le passage

Quand l'herbe lente
harcèle au bord les horizons

Plus profonds d'un présage
Plus graves d'une épreuve

Nous proférons des paroles
qui relatent la source.

Visage premier, p. 14

PASSAGE TO THE SOURCE

When the underbrush of time
gives us our path

When slow grass
touches the horizon with its fingers

Made more profound by an omen
Made graver by an ordeal

We utter words
that name the source.

L'ECLAIR ME TIENT

Je me déchiffre dans les marées
Le va-et-vient des ombres

Je me nomme
du nom des noyés
Tout s'écarte
Les sables rongent

Puis   d'un signe
Je me délie

Je suis lauriers et certitude

Le chant plane
L'éclair me tient.

Visage premier, p. 17

14

LIGHTNING CAPTURES ME

In the tides I find myself
in the ebb and flow of shadows

I become one
with the drowned
Everything vanishes
The sands gnaw
Then   with a sign
I break my bonds

I am laurels I am certainty

My poem soars
lightning captures me.

L'ECLAIR EST DANS LES CHAINES

L'aube ouvre ses mâchoires
sur l'abîme

L'éclair est dans les chaînes
Tous nos roseaux s'enlisent

Je ne suis que ce corps
qui s'enfonce comme une vrille

Je troue la terre de part en part.

Visage premier, p. 16

LIGHTNING IN CHAINS

Dawn opens its jaws
over the abyss

Lightning is in chains
All our reeds collapse

I am only a body
driving in like a gimlet

I pierce the earth from pole to pole

SILENCE A VIVRE

Certaines tombes ne jaunissent pas
Certaines fins multiplient le vertige
Certains départs s'adossent à la fraîche souffrance
Certains corps brulent à tous les âges du nôtre

Certaines paroles bouleversent
Tout le silence à vivre

Visage premier, p. 22

18

SILENCE TO LIVE

Certain tombs do not yellow with age
Certain deaths multiply our anguish
Certain departures bring on new suffering
Certain lives burn on through all our ages

Certain words shatter
All the silence we must live

DISCORDANCES

Je prononce
Pour mieux dire

TENEBRES
HIRONDELLE

Parce qu'elles se traversent
je dénombre les murailles

Je me serre contre l'ardoise
pour y graver poèmes

Et plonge dans les gouffres
pour embraser l'instant.

Visage premier, p. 40

DISCORDANCES

I pronounce   DARKNESS
To better say   SPARROW

Since they intersect
I destroy the walls

I cling to the slate
and there engrave my poems

And plunge into the chasms
to enkindle the instant.

POESIE I

Poésie
Tu nous mènes
vers la substance du monde

Lacérant en poèmes
le bandeau des mots

Rompant leur cartilage
Déconcant leurs lézardes

Questionnant la clairière
Cernant tout le brasier.

Visage premier, p. 54

POETRY I

Poetry
You lead us
to the substance of the world

Shredding into poems
the opacity of words

You break their gristle
You lay bare their cracks

You search the empty spaces
You encircle the fire.

POESIE II

Ce qui est plus que le mot
mais que le mot délivre

Ce qui est périssable
mais qui renaît devant

Ce qui sombre à foison
mais sans cesse se bâtit

Ce qui nous passe toujours
mais dont nous sommes semence

Ce qui a nom de vie
mais que les jours écartent

Ce qui est évidence
mais qui reste en suspens.

Visage premier, p. 55

POETRY II

What is more than the word
but delivered by the word

What dies
but rises again

What always surrenders
but is reborn

What grows beyond us
but is rooted in us

What we call life
but the days destroy

What is obvious
but remains obscure.

A QUOI JOUE-T-ON?

Que faisons-nous d'autre
que jardiner nos ombres,
Tandis qu'au loin
crépite et s'évade l'univers?

Que faisons-nous d'autre
que visiter le temps,
Tandis qu'au près
s'architecture notre mort?

Que faisons-nous d'autre
que rogner l'horizon,
Tandis qu'au loin
qu'au près ————————:

          le grand heurt.

Contre-chant, p. 9

WHAT GAME ARE WE PLAYING?

What else do we do
but tend our shadows,
While in the distance
the universe crackles
and slips our grasp?

What else do we do
but visit time,
While nearby
death carves its stone?

What else do we do
but narrow our horizon,
While far away
and nearby ————:

                    the great collision.

DEMARCHE I

J'ai tenté de joindre ma terre, à la terre;
Les mots, à la trame du silence;
Le large, au chant voilé.

Tenté de dire la rencontre possible,
Dégager le lieu de la nasse des refuges;
Fléchir la parole, jusqu'à la partager.

Puis, saluer celle-là,
Plus affranchie que nous:
Mort,
notre très certaine!

Pierre de touche, qui déroute l'épisode;
Compagne, qui retimbre la durée.

Celle-là,
dont l'image abolit les frontières,
Rétablit, ici même, notre face commune,
Et recentre, en ce monde,
tous nos temps dissipés.

Contre-chant, p. 11

STEP I

I tried to join earth to my earth;
My words to the cunning of silence;
Open sea to a sail-draped hymn.

Tried to say the encounter was possible,
To untangle a place from the snares of refusals;
To bend my words until they could be shared.

Then, to greet her,
More free than us,
Death,
Our promised one!

Touchstone that changes our story's course
Companion who sets the instant in motion.

She
whose image abolishes borders
Recaptures our common face
And retrieves, in this world,
all our lost hours.

SURGIR DU MOT

Parfois le mot
bouscule les grilles du langage

Parfois le mot
emporte et chevauche ma durée

Parfois le mot
échappe à la férule des mots

Parfois   Je deviens
ce que j'ai nommé

Alors
                              la VIE!
Parfois

Contre-chant, p. 28

30

THE SURGING WORD

Sometimes the word
rattles the cages of language

Sometimes the word
captures an instant from the flow of time

Sometimes the word
escapes the rule of words

Sometimes   I become
what I have named

Then

                    LIFE!

Sometimes

SANS L'EVIDENCE DU FRUIT

Jusqu'à l'ultime transparence,
L'ombre rusera avec nos vies.

Jusqu'à l'ultime transparence,
Les minutes rançonnent,
Les rêts se multiplient.

Jusqu'à l'ultime transparence,
et même par effraction:

Nous retracerons l'étoile,
Nous arracherons leur peau aux mirages,
Nous creuserons le champ ——
Sans l'évidence du fruit...

Contre-chant, p. 33

32

EYES BLIND TO THE FRUIT

Until the ultimate transparence,
Shadows will deceive our lives.

Until the ultimate transparence,
Minutes will buy us time,
Intrigues will multiply.

Until the ultimate transparence,
even with violence:

We'll comb the sky for stars,
We'll tear the skin from mirages
We'll dig up the field ——
Our eyes blind to its fruit . . .

CONTRE-ALLÉES

J'accours au large.
Je disperse mes saisons.
L'océan borde mes os.
L'espace me réfléchit.

Puis, avide des bouches de la terre,
Otage fasciné,
Me revoici:

> *A l'assaut des remparts*
> *Au parvis des rencontres,*
> *Suspendu aux gorges du présent,*
> *Mordant à son ombre, à ses fruits!*

Mais   vois,
J'accours au large.
Je disperse mes saisons.
L'océan borde mes os.

L'espace me réfléchit.

Contre-chant, p. 35

COUNTER-MOVEMENTS

I rush to open seas.
I scatter my seasons.
Oceans border my bones.
Spaces reflect my image.

Then, eager for the mouths of the earth,
A wide-eyed hostage,
Here I am again:

> At the seige of the ramparts,
> At the brink of encounters,
> Suspended over the gorges of the present,
> Biting at its shadow, at its fruit!

But   look,
I rush to open seas
I scatter my seasons.
Oceans border my bones.

Spaces reflect my image.

AVANT

C'est avant ta naissance
                    que se hasarde ta vie

C'est avant ton regard
                    que résident tes images

C'est avant ta parole
                    que repose ta voix

C'est avant ton pas
                    que progresse ta route

            C'est bien avant ta mort
            que se fomente ta fin.

Contre-chant, p. 43

36

BEFORE

Before your birth
     your life takes a chance

Before your glance
     your images are shaped

Before your word
     resides your voice

Before your step
     your road is laid out

     And well before your death
     you begin to die.

PAROLE

Je te connais, Parole,
Si patiemment construite,
Avec tes arceaux
Plus tenaces que nos voix.

Je te salue, Parole,
Délivrée d'être dite,
Qui nous tire de nous-mêmes
Comme cerf hors des bois.

Je te cerne, Parole,
Te veux proie et docile;
Tu mûris bleue et libre
Et m'invente à ton tour.

Si, jaloux de ton faîte,
Je te gravis, Parole,
Mon ombre provisoire
S'annule à chaque détour.

Contre-chant, p. 56

38

WORDS

Words, I know you well,
So patiently constructed,
With arches
More tenacious than our voices.

I salute you, Words,
Freed from being spoken,
You bring us out of ourselves,
Like a stag out of his forest.

I pursue you, Words,
Eager to harness my prey;
You ripen blue and free
And capture me instead.

If, jealous of your peak,
I climb your mountain, Words,
My ephemeral shadow
Fades with every turn.

L'INSTANT I

L'instant sème.

Mais nos terres l'éconduisent
Sans nommer sa fleur.

Ainsi se perdent
les moissons
Ainsi s'embourbent
les songes
Ainsi chavirent
les jours

Ainsi périt,
l'instant.

Contre-chant, p. 59

INSTANT I

The instant casts a seed.

But our soil silently rejects it
Never naming the flower.

And thus
        the harvest is lost
        the dreams become enmired
        the days run aground
And so
        the instant dies.

AMARRE, NOTRE LIBERTE

Le jour parfois s'enlise,
Bouche nos avenues,
Crible demain de rocs,
Se raidit sur nos prés.

Vivons alors d'un visage,
Souvenons-nous de l'arche partagée.

Nos mots résorbent les portes d'ombre
Nos liens délivrent la liberté.

Contre-chant, p. 72

CHAINS, OUR FREEDOM

Sometimes days collapse,
And block our avenues,
Scatter tomorrow with rocks,
Grow stiff upon our meadows,

We must then draw life from a face,
We must remember the arches we share.

Our words engulf the shadowed doors,
Our bonds set freedom free.

ANNIE SALAGER

ANNIE SALAGER:
THE DISTILLING EYE

Annie Salager does not distrust language. Words are not violently pushed and shoved, or forced into new relationships with one another in order to create a new experience. With Salager, new experiences are created by seeing the world in new ways, by viewing reality through what Andrée Chedid calls "l'autre regard," the "other eye." Rather than alter her medium of communication, Salager wants to alter her faculties of perception, and then communicate that perception through a language which we will find comfortable. The prose poem entitled **The Glazed Pot** (p. 61) illustrates this process. Here the various furnishings of a room—a chest-of-drawers, a lamp, a pitcher, a mirror—become distilled into their essence—textures, shapes, colors, rhythms— when seen through the mind/eye of the poet. We must not view objects "face to face," says Salager, but rather we should view our relationship to them, "keeping them in focus, looking beyond them."

It is this process of "seeing" that is all-important in Annie Salager. In her eyes, pebbles become "roads of unwoven intrigues," poems are transformed into "naked knives," and the ocean is seen as "an abyss of timeless stairways." When described by the eye of the mind, the various moods and moments of the poet take on a greater intensity. And in this connection, one should be aware of the importance of images of windows and eyes in Salager's poetry, because they are almost invariably associated with this faculty of vision. The moods that Salager shares with us vary widely, from the feeling of ecstasy invoked in her by her children: "for them only, the rivers of my body create oceans and open spaces," to the confused frustration of "Always I change and stay the same," to the anguish and abnegation of "I cannot speak to you. You cannot hear me . . . Words drop out like lead marbles."

In addition to the concern for inventing new perceptions which much of Salager's poetry reflects, there is also a concern in many other poems for rendering a more or less photographic representation of reality, with only the slightest hint of conceptual transformation. In the **Série de portraits sur le vif** ("Series of Lifelike Portraits"), which begins the collection entitled **La Femme-Buisson,** for example, there is a lengthy description of a "worker attached to his jack-hammer." However, in spite of the

45

attractions of the concrete world, Salager is still fascinated by darkness, by the abyss, and by those areas of human experience that are unexplainable in rational terms, those areas that cannot be sharply focused and "photographed" by the mere eye. These are areas impenetrable except through poetry. These are also areas that we hesitiate to enter, because there we find only darkness and the self. Alone in the poem, with only ourselves to encounter, we are afraid: "the poem appears like a puddle of dark blood" *("le poème surgit comme une flaque de sang sombre").* Salager does not, then, revel in darkness and the self like the more courageous Thérèse Plantier (to be discussed later); yet, like the latter, she represents the unknown by associating images of sea and water with darkness, and she describes her voyages to the inner self by images of boats and vessels. In the poem **Vagues . . . une fois encore** ("Waves, once again"), a ship (i.e., a poet, a reader) becomes one with night, and the fruit of this union is an intensified ability to "see":

> groaning ship set adrift
> your mast has nailed you to the night
> your eyes multiply
> your body flourishes under the labor of
> the waters

> *Gémis gémis navire sans attache*
> *ton mât t'a cloué à la nuit*
> *tes yeux se multiplient*
> *ton corps fleurit sous le labour des eaux*
>
> **(Histoire pour le jour, p. 17)**

However, Salager's attitude towards darkness and the unknown is always ambivalent. In the poem **Night of the Poem, Perfect Love,** (p. 53) when night kneels down beside her, she hears "murmurs and luring voices," but she hesitates to enter the world of darkness because she is unfamiliar with it, and therefore afraid of it. She has never learned to "weave its threads." Later in the poem, however, she regrets not having entered the world of darkness, she regrets knowing so little of how "night opens its hands." This ambivalence is seen again in **In the Dark** (p. 57) where the poet, although she has extinguished her lamp, still sees the "world's fires burn brightly." As a poet who wants to enter her own private world of darkness, but is unable to ignore the "cries from the other side of the earth," the "murders and corruption," she realizes that she is a mosaic of different beings, each with a different hunger, a different need to be fulfilled:

46

so many famished beings have risen within me
their ugly features embedded in my genes
so many who refuse consolation.

tant d'êtres se sont levés en moi avec famine
avec leur sale mine dans l'héritage
tant, qui veulent n'être pas consolés.

(Histoire pour le jour, p. 44)

Her hunger for darkness can only be satisfied by the poem, and
yet the poem is often only "fragments of birds, situated no-
where." In the poem **A Certain Hatred of Poetry** (p. 63), her
own voice becomes "lips overflowing with nothingness," and she
laments her "imagination always overflowing." The inherent
danger in poetry is that it leads us into a world where words are
no longer secure; and, for that reason, we are no longer secure:
"your words lead to places where they themselves do not exist"
("tes paroles conduisent où elles n'existent pas").

Although many of Salager's poems betray a confusion as to what
the role of the poet should be, whether to record the dynamics
of the self or the dynamics of reality, we do not see an anguished
struggle between the self and reality that we do in, for example,
Denise Grappe. One has the feeling that, no matter what terrain
Salager explores, even if it arouses fear, it was still worth exploring.
It takes courage to explore the night, to "reach one's hands" into
the world where "words tangle with flesh among imaginary vines,"
or to plunge "into the black waters." But once the poet has
overcome the fear, she is rewarded by a vision that penetrates
beyond reality:

At night I dream; dreams that the cliffs
of dawn destroy . . . But then, what a
vision over the sea's horizon!

La nuit, je rêve; des rêves que déchire
la falaise de l'aube . . . Mais quel coup
d'oeil alors sur l'horizon de mer!

(Histoire pour le jour, p. 12)

Her plunges into darkness, although they shut off the light from
the outside world, create an inner light by which she can see into
the dark and hidden corners of her own self:

If I bathe in the night
my eyes will invade my body.

Si je me baigne dans la nuit
mes yeux envahiront mon corps.
(**La Femme-buisson,** p. 25)

ANNIE SALAGER

Born in Paris, Annie Salager now resides in Lyon where she teaches Spanish. In 1973 she received the Louise Labé prize for her collection, **La Femme-Buisson.** Thus far, she has published the following books of poetry:

> **La Nuit introuvable** (Henneuse, 1961)
> **Présent de sable** (Chambelland, 1964)
> **Histoire pour le jour** (Seghers, 1968)
> **Dix profils sur la toile** (Henneuse, 1971)
> **La Femme-Buisson** (Saint-Germain-des-Prés, 1973)

Poème
couteaux nus
qui vous feraient saigner jusqu'au réveil
J'ai plongé mon bras dans la nuit:
des mots s'enchevêtraient aux chairs
parmi d'imaginaires lianes.

Histoire pour le jour, p. 11

50

Poem
naked knives
that make you bleed until you awake
My hands reached into the night:
words tangled with flesh
among imaginary vines.

NUIT DU POEME, PARFAIT AMOUR

La nuit si lente à accomplir ses rites
il me semble
——— mais est-ce possible ———
proche très proche s'agenouille.

Murmures, provocations, circuits
j'aborde avec crainte
——— n'ai pas appris à filer la laine ———
la rumeur de ce fuseau.

La lune s'enfouit dans ses plaids de nuages
tout s'inonde ici
moutons qui passent ne cessent de passer
dans la douceur du nombre.

Monde de l'étouffant, visages clos,
fatigues sur la jambe du vide lancées
depuis le sommeil des formes
monde immodéré toujours trahi.

Sommeil posé sur l'établi des rêves
viborne des lointains intérieurs
faits de glace quand on les croit de feu
de glace et de feu.

NIGHT OF THE POEM, PERFECT LOVE

It seems
—— but can it be ——
that night kneels down close by
and celebrates its slow ritual.

Whispers, luring voices, hesitations
I touch with fear
—— having never learned to spin the wool ——
the humming of the spindle.

The moon snuggles into its blanket of clouds
Here everything bathes in its own light
the passing sheep do not cease to pass
in the sweetness of their number.

Stifling world, closed faces,
legs of the void thrown into weariness
and then shapes asleep
intemperate world always deceived.

Sleep placed on the workbench of dreams
bridge to distant interiors
made of ice when we think they're made of fire
of ice and fire.

J'y endors le parapet des prairies marines
pour écouter le vent descendre
ceinture aventureuse
qui me fait gémir de si mal savoir.

De si mal savoir comment la nuit ouvre ses mains
ouvre ses mains
mais c'est pour disparaître
et murmurer très proche
plus loin.

Histoire pour le jour, p. 18

There I lull to sleep the ramparts of ocean meadows
to hear the wind pick up
the adventurous embrace
that makes me moan to know so little.

To know so little how night opens its hands
opens its hands
but it's only to disappear
and murmur ever closer
far away.

DANS LE NOIR

J'éteins. Le monde brille de ses feux.
J'écoute. Il y a des cris de l'autre côté de la terre
des meurtres des saletés
et nul repos sinon la mort
plantée en écharde.
La vie ressemble à l'être sans visage
qui nous tient dans ses bras
sans que jamais le jour se fasse
et bien qu'il passe.
Cependant gronde le soleil fluvial d'Amérique latine
semblable aux poèmes d'amour de Neruda
à l'orpailleur Nicolás Guillén . . .
Par là j'aime par là je souffre
tant d'êtres se sont levés en moi avec famine
avec leur sale mine dans l'héritage
tant, qui veulent n'être pas consolés.
Je navigue sur leur vaisseau
qui court la mer brumeuse et ronde
trop vaste trop nue.
Le monde brille
mon enfant qui pleures dans le noir
la vie ressemble . . .

Histoire pour le jour, p. 44

IN THE DARK

I douse the lamp. The world is bright with fire.
I listen. Cries from the other side of the earth
murders and corruption
and no repose other than death
planted like a splinter.
Life resembles a faceless being
that holds us in its arms
while days pass by
and never show their light.
Yet like the love poems of Neruda
like the gold panner Nicolas Guillen
Latin America pours out a river of sun . . .
Here I love there I suffer
so many famished beings have risen within me
their ugly features imbedded in my genes
so many who refuse consolation.
I sail on their ship
over the round and misty ocean
too vast too empty.
The world burns brightly
my child crying in the dark
life resembles . . .

MER

Sculptée dans les cryptes des gisants
mer que l'on édifie
mer en abîme d'escaliers immémoriaux creusés de notre
      chair de pierre
racine de mandragore dont ne cesse plus le gémissement
      et que l'on enterre
lieu du silence ou s'abreuve notre mort, notre reconnais-
      sance
miroir aussi de toutes portes vides, fidèle au temps
absente, comme la forme obscure d'une saison première
      qui s'écoule de nuage en nuage
et nous impose de l'aimer sous ce manteau défleuri pareil
      au sourire de lieux réduits en cendres
mer indifférente et propice
mer patiente accumulée
surpeuplement que n'emporte aucune marée, où meurt
      l'espace
mais aussi miracle
mer des nuits obscures de la mystique
mais aussi miracle
qui sous nos yeux s'ordonne et meurt
s'ordonne meurt et s'ordonne.

Histoire pour le jour, p. 49

OCEAN

Carved in the crypts of the dead
ocean we have conjured
abyss of timeless stairways hollowed from our stony flesh
mandrake whose ceaseless moaning root we bury
space of silence where death, our recognition, comes to drink
mirror of all the empty doors, faithful to time,
absent, like the vague shape of a young season that flows
      from cloud to cloud
and makes us love it beneath a flowerless cape
      like the smile of places reduced to ashes
ocean indifferent and fertile
ocean patient and abundant
teeming with life that no tide can wash away, where spaces
      die
but also miracle
ocean of the mystics' dark night
that comes and dies in our presence
that comes and dies and comes.

LE POT DE FAIENCE

Les ferrures de la commode, la lampe de cuivre, les filets d'or de l'abat-jour, le vieux miroir aux ors brunis, le pot-à-eau couleur crème, court et ventru, orné d'une guirlande de fleurs roses, tout cela, un mur blanc, grossièrement crépi sur des pierres visibles à la geographie des craquelures qui le recouvrent, tout cela, ce matin, forme l'espace où le réel vient prendre, comme un bon mot, comme une colle, comme un mensonge prennent où ne prennent pas.

Brillant du cuivre, de la faïence, du bois de la commode, du miroir. Couleurs jaune, brune, beige, rose, et du blanc. Texture et forme, couleur et rythme, posés, affirmés dans une nécessité rigoureuse, comme de longtemps appelée, de loin venue par des hasards vers du hasard seulement. Opacité du réel, impénétrable, pâte de l'imaginaire.

Non pas face aux objets mais, par rapport à eux, dans un angle de vision aigu.

Histoire pour le jour, p. 50

60

THE GLAZED POT

The brasswork on the dresser, the copper lamp, the threads of gold on the lamp-shade, the old gilt-edged mirror, the cream colored pitcher, short and portly, strung with a garland of pink flowers, all this, a blank wall, roughly plastered with rocks showing through its cracked landscape, all this, this morning, forms the space where the real takes hold, like a good word, like a lie, like glue take hold or do not.

Brilliance of copper, of glaze, of the wood of the dresser, of the mirror. Colors, yellow, brown, beige, pink, and white. Texture and shape, color and rhythm, held out, affirmed by a need to be, long awaited, brought from afar by chance, moving only toward chance. Opacity of the real, impenetrable, putty of the imagination.

Not face to face with objects, but keeping them in focus, looking beyond them.

UNE CERTAINE HAINE DE LA POESIE

. . . Et toujours l'imaginaire déborde.
Il faut recommencer, tendre la corde.

Limaille d'oiseau située nulle part
je t'inventai une aile, blanche sœur des hasards!

Cailloux, ô mes chemins, trames inachevées
j'ai la passion du vivre et des années

dont le fruit se dérobe en un compte à rebours,
où le combat des hommes s'enfièvre de détours

j'ai la passion multiple de leurs lendemains
j'ai leur soif et leur honte j'ai leur impatience pour pain.

Pour lutte, pour outil, pour amour ce poème
qui me défait, se détourne et se trahit lui-même . . .

O lèvres qu'un néant deborde et durable sourire
O durable sourire ô lèvres qu'un néant déborde.

Histoire pour le jour, p. 61

A CERTAIN HATRED OF POETRY

. . . Imagination always overflowing.
I must start again, tighten the strings.

Fragments of birds situated nowhere
I invent a wing for you, pale sister of chance!

Pebbles, O my roads of unwoven intrigues
I have a passion for life and for years

whose fruits disappear one by one,
where men fight feverishly over details

I hunger even more for their tomorrows
I have their thirst and shame their impatience for bread.

My struggle my tool my love, this poem
that destroys me, turns around and betrays itself . . .

O lips overlfowing with nothingness O stubborn smile
O stubborn smile O lips overflown with nothingness.

Avec les mêmes mains dont j'écris cette ligne
avec les mêmes mains que toi
avec les mêmes mains dont on salue et on étreint
dont on calme caresse écoute
avec les mêmes mains qui se répandent comme une eau
ou qui s'effrittent miette à miette
non pas faites pour gants ou photos
ni manucure ou séchage à l'air chaud
mais pour se fermer avec rage devant les murs trop
        haut des choses établies
devant le gros gibier de la machine économique
devant les vies glissant de tout leur poids à prix
        fixe vers elles
avec les mêmes mains palpant les pièces de soierie
d'un mot exact d'un monde juste ô rêveries
je mêle aux tiennes mes frontières.

La Femme-Buisson, p. 21

With the same hands that I write this line
the same hands as yours
the same hands that say hello and embrace
that soothe and listen and caress
the same hands that spread like water
or that crumble away bit by bit
not made for gloves or photos
or manicures or nail polish
but for clenching with rage before the towers of established
        things
before the thick hide of the economic machine
before the lives that slide with all the weight of fixed
        prices toward them
with the same hands that fondle pieces of silk
of a pointed word from a just world O dreams
I touch my borders with yours.

Souvenez-vous,
les rendez-vous manqués à l'horloge immobile

Souvenez-vous,
malles du vent au visage inconnu

Vous n'aviez rien prévu ni songé à l'usure

Vous pensiez pourtant aux malentendus
et comme il suffirait d'ouvrir à deux battants les
      mots
pour lire ce visage qui surgirait parfois à la vitre
      éphémère

Tout semblait difficile et possible, alors,

Considérez
les rendez-vous manqués à l'horloge immobile

La Femme-Buisson, p. 22

66

Remember,
the meetings we missed at the silent clock

Remember,
the undecipherable messages borne in the wind

You didn't foresee how the years would wear us down

Yet you did think of the misunderstandings
and when it would suffice to open the
gates of words
to read this face that sometimes appeared behind an
ephemeral window

It all seemed difficult and possible, then

So think about
those meetings we missed at the silent clock

Pas beaucoup d'espace sur ma terre
bien peu de fenêtres pour ma maison
et le froid de la vitre à mon front
il y a derrière bien peu d'horizon

Pas beaucoup d'espace sur ma terre
ni beaucoup d'espoir ni beaucoup d'oiseaux
s'il advient qu'un ciel s'illumine
pour chasser l'ombre des barreaux

Il n'y a vraiment pas beaucoup d'espace.

La Femme-buisson, p. 27

Not much space on my earth
not many windows for my house
the cold pane at my forehead
there is little horizon beyond

Not much space on my earth
not much hope nor many birds
if only the sun could brighten the sky
to chase away the shadows of the bars

There is really not much space.

MALAISE

Je ne peux te parler. Tu ne peux pas m'entendre. Mur après mur la pièce où nous nous trouvons tous les deux rétrécit. Chaque détail se colle à mon regard, pèse, chaque geste trébuche, arrête le temps. Les mots prononcés sont des billes de plomb qui se perdent. Quelque chose souffle derrière un masque, va et vient entre nous, cherche en tatonnant sa circulation, puis nous rejette vialemment contre les murs en occupant la place où nous étions assis, et où deux étrangers maintenant nous regardent.

La Femme-buisson, p. 32

70

SICKNESS

I cannot speak to you. You cannot hear me. Wall
after wall the room that encloses us shrinks. Each
detail clings to my eyes, weighs heavy, each gesture
jolts, stops the flow of time. Words drop out like lead
marbles. Something hisses behind a mask, moves back
and forth between us, gropes its way, then throws us
violently against the walls and occupies the place
where we were seated, and where two strangers now
gaze at us.

DENISE GRAPPE

DENISE GRAPPE:
THE VOICE OF THE SILENT HEART

The poetry of Denise Grappe records a bitter struggle between the 'I' of the poem and reality, a struggle which is not resolved, but only temporarily suspended by moments of peace and silence. These moments are created by the poet when, through the act of poetic transformation, she changes her own identity, and thereby elevates herself above the struggle.

Grappe builds her metaphorical structure around two important images: the knife and the wound. The knife is constantly associated with reality, and the result of the knife's action, the wound, is associated with the "I" of the poem. The poet's overall view of reality, a view embodied in the two above images, is frightfully pessimistic:

> Are executioners and victims
> All we have on earth?
>
> *N'existe-t-il sur terre*
> *Que bourreaux et victimes?*
> **(Durée arrachée, p. 11)**

Rounding out this dreary picture are images of black sunflowers, cold embraces, flowers and birds shivering with dead colors, and paths strewn with thorns. Constantly, one sees grimacing faces, hears agonized cries, and witnesses bloody massacres. Her allusions to crowns of thorns, scourges, Calvary, crucified victims and sacrificial lambs all have a distinctly Christian tone,[1] but we need not place Grappe's poetry in a Christian context to appreciate the power of these images. They are a means of representing the poetic voice as a victim of the destructive forces of reality. Along with this self-concept as martyr comes a note of bitter cynicism:

> Thoughts crushed by your own power
> Why don't you burst open
> Like a hemorrhage
> And deliver us anew
> To pale innocence
>
> *Pensées écrasées sous leur propre pesée*
> *Pourquoi ne sortez-vous*
> *Comme hémorragie*

[1] See *Crue,* pp. 8, 12, 16, 30, 37, and *Durée arrachée*, pp. 32, 36, 38, 43.

> *Pour nous redonner neufs*
> *A l'innocence pâle*
> **(Durée arrachée,** p. 12)

For Grappe life is a delicate balance; destructive forces are held in equilibrium, but only by other tensions which are in opposition themselves:

> Frail balance
> In question
> Each day righted
> By the knives
> Of memories
>
> *Frêle équilibre*
> *En question*
> *Remis chaque jour*
> *Par les couteaux*
> *Du souvenir*
> **(Durée arrachée,** p. 11)

The part of the poet most vulnerable to these destructive forces is the emotions, and quite often she speaks of the heart, seat of the emotions, as needing to be closed off to the outside world. It is necessary to put armor around the heart:

> I arm my heart
> In the deaf pain
> of a cast of concrete
>
> *J'arme mon coeur*
> *Dans la sourde douleur ·*
> *d'une coulée de béton*
> **(Durée arrachée,** p. 24)

Elsewhere, Grappe speaks of "the patched-up silence of a heart" *("le silence rapiécé d'un coeur")* and of "a padlocked heart" *("un coeur cadenassé")*.

The impulse for purity and a return to lost innocence—one cannot help thinking that these are among the most secret wishes of the poet. But time after time these dreams of innocence are cut to shreds by the blades of reality. In the following poem images of purity and innocence are succeeded by images of destruction by a dagger:

A bird
A puff of wind
A child
Cross my horizon

A despairing wait

A dagger
Hesitates
Then
Slowly
Penetrates
The ebony
Of a tear

Un oiseau
Un coup de vent
Un enfant
Traversent mon horizon

Une attente
Un désespoir

Coup de poignard
Hésitant
Pénètre
Longuement
L'ébène
D'une larme

(Durée arrachée, p. 40)

Knifeblades, honed on reality, are always ready to cut into their sacrificial victims:

Blades that hone themselves
On the edge of reality
How deep
Will you cut
The offered flesh

Lames qui s'aiguisent
Au tranchant du réel
Jusqu'où
Taillerez-vous
La chair offerte

(Durée arrachée, p. 11)

75

Spring, the season of rebirth, is, for Grappe, a time for death:

> The Spring has the taste of
> A massacre
> Part of the sky has fallen

> *Ce printemps a goût de*
> *Saccage*
> *Un pan de ciel a basculé*
>
> **(Durée arrachée, p. 27)**

For Grappe, beauty is often associated with death: "I contemplate my death in your beautiful nakedness." Elsewhere, beauty is described as "monsters from the depths." Beauty is not permanent, will not withstand the ravages of time, always succumbs to death:

> Hemming my window
> The discreet odor of
> Death that
> Overcomes all beauty

> *Ourlant ma fenêtre*
> *Cette discrète odeur de*
> *Mort qui*
> *Double toute beauté*
>
> **(Durée arrachée, p. 35)**

Grappe's poetry is, above all, a poetry of tension and dissonance. The dissonance can come from unusual juxtapositions of emotional and mechanical situations perhaps best illustrated in the poem which begins "showers of sparks" (p. 91). In the poem an emotional outpour and excitement clashes with the machinery of banks and offices groaning and screeching in the background. In the poem which begins "I hammer syllables" (p. 101), the words of the poet are reflected by blood and mire; and in the one which begins "Wombs that shelter," the eye and the hand celebrate "discordant rites" in wombs of "calm despair."

The poet is able to overcome this tension and dissonance, this struggle between herself and reality, by becoming one with reality. This process, which one might describe as the ingestion of reality into the poetic consciousness, enables the poet to create a moment of peace, a temporary hiatus, in her ongoing struggle with reality. In a poem describing the process of breaking free from this struggle, **Arrache tes amarres** ("Break your chains"), Grappe counsels us to jump with both feet onto a bed of hot coals, to kiss the fire on the lips, to drink our blood, and to call, at the same time, the sun and the ice onto our bodies. This way we will be "forever invincible." In another poem, she describes, in sacramental terms, the drinking of blood from a running wound. In still another poem, Grappe talks of becoming "wind, sky, tree, tear, laughter and blood." Finally, the poet expresses her desire to hear "strange cries that crack like strips of hippopotamus hide, biting and shredding my flesh" *("des cris étranges qui claquent telles des lanières d'hippopotames écorchés arrachant ma chair lambeau par lambeau").*

The moments of peace and tranquility, which are brought about by the poet's becoming one with tormenting reality, do not come often. Sometimes the transforming word fails to bring about this oneness. In the piece entitled **Rite of Spring,** (p. 93) words are only a "blind whiteness of sounds" that do not have the strength to free the poet from "vacuum cleaners and other vampires." Sometimes words betray the poet herself, and break away from her conscious control, and become embedded in reality, thus becoming the instrument of her destruction:

> Words take on a reality
> More horrible than the wound
>
> *Les mots se doublent d'une réalité*
> *Plus affreuse que la blessure*
> **(Durée arrachée,** p. 43)

Words are sometimes traitors:

> Words, yesterday's
> Offering
> Traps today
>
> *Mots hier*
> *Offerts*
> *Pièges, aujourd'hui*
> **(Durée arrachée,** p. 35)

But at certain instants words have the power to "force open a clenched fist." At certain times Grappe rises above her struggle, as the poem which begins "The labyrinth untangles" (p. 97) illustrates. Here Grappe, in the manner of Chedid, records a "privileged moment" when the corridors of the labyrinth unwind and she touches the "ultimate point." But even though at times she reaches these moments of "consummate perfection," she is dismayed by the very fact that they are perfect, and ephemeral, and the experience of this "perfect" instant makes her want to fill "all the hours" behind her.

DENISE GRAPPE

Denise Grappe, born in Strasbourg in 1926 and now living in Luxembourg, was a founder of a group of activist Alsatian writers called the *"Conseil des Ecrivains d'Alsace"* in 1971. In addition to her poems, Denise Grappe has published a volume of stories. Her published works include:

> Durée arrachée (Ed. de la Grisière, 1969)
> Bois de mémoire (Saint-Germain-des-Prés, 1971)
> Crue suivi de Poème pour X (Saint-Germain-des-
> Prés, 1972)
> 9 x 7 Microcosmes (Chambelland, 1975)

Ton visage entrevu
Au coeur
Me creuse

Plus bas
Ronge
La loutre

Durée arrachée, p. 26

Your face glimpsed
In the heart
Drains me

Farther down
Gnaws
The otter

J'ai joint mes lèvres
A celles ouvertes
    de ta chair
Sous le couteau

J'ai reçu
Ta mort bue
    En sacrement

Durée arrachée, p. 32

I joined my lips
To the open lips
    of your flesh
Against the knife

I drank
Your death
    A sacrament

Pourquoi le desert convulsé
Dignité austère
Qui se drape
Dans un habit de brume

Pourquoi ne pas être
Un dernier feu de joie
Torche résineuse
Qui sans laisser de cendres
Se consume
Eclairant les ténèbres
D'un éclat oublié

Durée arrachée, p. 21

Why the convulsions in the desert
Austere dignity
That drapes itself
In a coat of mist

Why not be
One last fire of joy
A resinous torch
That consumes itself
Without leaving ashes
Lighting the darkness
With a forgotten flame

Ta nudité
flagellée
Sous le
Regard

J'ai contemplé
Ma mort
Dans ta
Nudité
               Belle

Crue, p. 12

Your nakedness
scourged
By a
Stare

I contemplate
My death
In your
          Beautiful
Nakedness

Vous savez la beauté
Monstres des profondeurs
Qui fendent la noirceur
Des eaux
Ramenant leurs corps nus
En surface
Pour fixer la lumière
De leurs yeux qui ont vu

Ces yeux-là, vôtres, j'ai
fixés

Crue, p. 13

You know beauty
Monsters from the depths
Who split the blackness
Of the water
Bringing naked bodies
To the surface
To fix the light
Of eyes that have seen

Those eyes, your eyes,
I have fixed their gaze

Du soleil des poitrines
                              jailliront
Les buissons d'étincelles
Des mots foudroyés

Entre banques bureaux
Grincent les rouages

Crue, p. 19

Showers of sparks
From electrified words
                        burst forth
From a sun-filled breast

Between banks and offices
Tired gears groan

SACRE DU PRINTEMPS

Blanc aveugle
Des sons
J'attends votre éclatement

Assez puissants n'êtes
Pour me délivrer
Des aspirateurs
Et autres monstres vampires

J'attends
Temps mort
Votre révélation

Sillons
Je vous accepte
Dans la perfection
D'une rouge incantation

Crue, p. 23

92

RITE OF SPRING

Blind whiteness
Of sounds
I await your explosion

You are not strong enough
To free me
From vacuum cleaners
And other vampires

In dead time
I await
Your revelation

Furrows
I accept you
In the perfection
Of a red incantation

Après-midi glauques
Silence de l'eau froissée
Trouble qui se referme
Vide peuplé de possibles
Pesanteur incertaine
Pourquoi
Ne basculais-je
De l'autre côté
Du côté
Des jeux d'eau
Arachnéens

Géométrie et poésie
Inconditionnelle perfection
Je vous rêvai

Crue, p. 27

Glaucous afternoons
Water silent and troubled
Disturbance closing over
Void peopled with possibility
Uncertain weight
Why didn't I waver
From the other side
The side
Where spiders play games
On the water

Geometry and poetry
Of absolute perfection
I invented you in a dream

Labyrinthe s'ordonne
Couloirs se défont
Au creuset de l'instant

Vie en suspens
Au-delà
Tombée, touché
Le point ultime

Reste à
Combler le
Temps dépassé

Crue, p. 29

The labyrinth untangles
Corridors uncoil
In the crucible of the instant

Life suspended
In the hereafter
Fallen, the ultimate point
Touched

Only time past
remains
to be filled

FILLE

Belle
De toutes les lèvres
Carminées
Qui fleurissent
Ton corps

Crue, p. 43

GIRL

Pretty
with all the crimson
Lips
That flower
Your body

Je martèle
D'acier
Les syllabes

Sang et boue
Dessinent
L'étoile
De l'éclatement

Crue, p. 46

I hammer
Syllables
With steel

Blood and mire
Reflect
The star
Of the explosion

Matrices
Du calme désespoir
Journées
Habillées
De chair où
L'oeil et la main
Célèbrent
Des rites
Désaccordés

Crue, p. 47

Wombs
of quiet despair
Days
Dressed
In flesh where
Eye and hand
Celebrate
Discordant
Rites

MARIE-FRANCOISE PRAGER

Marie-Françoise Prager's poetry focuses on the relationship between her inner consciousness and the details of her immediate surroundings. Because of this preoccupation, her poetry often treats perception—the mind/eye turning upon and contemplating itself. We do not see any brilliantly variegated imagery snatched from the objective world and transformed as in Annie Salager or Yvonne Caroutch. Nor do we see her seize upon the outside world as does Thérèse Plantier and violently disrupt the order of the mosaic. Poetic transformation does occur in Prager; and it is a transformation of the most immediately accessible material: the body and its sensations, the mind and its visions.

Prager's voice speaks to us from a severely restricted space, as if the poet were confined to a room with only herself and a few elemental surroundings. There are no dazzling colors or fire as in Andrée Chedid; the sun is never present; only the moon shines, and its glow "fuses into plates / like stiff baroque." Prager's world is a world of flat surfaces, muted tones, and dull edges. Since her outside world is so flat, so inanimate, so neutral and unobtrusive, Prager focuses her attention on the fantasies and obsessions of her inner mind, which find poetic expression testifying to her dream. Frequently, the subject of her dream is death, as evidenced by numerous references to tombs, cemeteries and mummies. In the poem which begins "I think about the dead woman" (p. 113), Prager speaks of the infinite powers of the dream to reflect back upon and re-create the dreamer: "I am . . . the object / dreaming of dreaming the object." In this line, the dreamer and the dream are like two facing mirrors whose reciprocating reflection creates an infinity of images. The ultimate way to apprehend this dream is by becoming the poem itself: "I am the poem in a tomb." And, although she herself is the dead woman in this poem, she rises above death by the very consciousness of being dead. In the poem which begins "I want to live an absurd dream" (p. 117), Prager reiterates her desire to approximate the dream itself. In this poem, and in others, the approximation of the dream is often associated with imagery likening her to a bird: "I want . . . to mimick the gait of a crippled bird / throw my wing . . . to the gnawed moon." In a prose poem, Prager describes a bird who approaches and lands on her shoulders:

I feel the matter of its wings melt into
my contours, I know the bird is the same
size as me.

*Je sens la matière des ailes se fondre en
mes contours, je sais que l'oiseau est de
ma taille.*

(Narcose, p. 70)

To become one with her dream it seems that Prager needs to
overcome the confines of the body: "Flesh: clumsy and un-
predictable that follows the whims of liquid blood all colored."
Although she is sometimes haunted by the body in her waking
hours *("l'épiderme me hante")*, the body itself may generate a
dream through which the body falls away:

. . . in the natural dream the surface
of the body dissolves; forbidden by
the excesses of my passion, the body
crumbles, it is no longer palpable.

*. . . dans le rêve naturel la surface du
corps se dissout; deféndu par l'excès
de ma passion le corps se ruine, il n'est
plus palpable.*

(Narcose, p. 72)

Once the surface of the body is dissolved, once "the aorta is
hidden," the poet is permitted to dream through her skin: *"vous
rêvez par la peau"* (p. 118).

The dream does not always bring pleasurable sensations; at times,
her dreams are more like nightmares. This is evidenced by
numerous references to beasts and monsters which occur in
Prager's poetry. The poet is never sure where her dream will take
her:

Through what detours will the
coachman of somnolence bring us home?

*Par quel circuit le cocher du
demi-sommeil nous laisse en place?*

(Narcose, p. 69)

But even though the dream sometimes confronts the poet with
the monsters of her existence, it also provides her with a life
which is more intense, more stimulating than the drab objects
which make up her world. In the poem which begins "in the

106

palm of my hand," (p. 111), the dream enables a "tender word" to become a loud shout. If, as in the prose poem which begins "Celebration of absence" (p. 127), Prager overcomes her fear of the nightmare and keeps the bird of the dream clutched tightly in her hand, she will then feel "a tiny heartbeat" of life.

With Prager, the most minute sparks, precious affirmations of life within a world of empty greyness, explode within the intense blackness of the dream and create life.

MARIE-FRANCOISE PRAGER

Marie-Françoise Prager, born of French parents in Amsterdam, now lives under treatment in Italy. Although her poetry remained for a long time unpublished, it was not, however, unrecognized. Well before 1966, when her first volume of poems was published, Gaston Bachelard, Roland Barthes and Jean Rousselot had all expressed their admiration for her poetry. Prager has contributed to the journal **Esprit.** She has published two volumes of poems:

> **Narcose** (Chambelland, 1966)
> **Rien ne se perd** (Chambelland, 1970)

Au creux de ma main
un diminutif hurlé
tel que dans la conque
le plan d'un labyrinthe
le refrain de vent
sur une mer sans ouïe
et de mémoire restreinte
j'ai gardé de ton souffle
et du menton soumis
l'obsédante empreinte.

Narcose, p. 11

In the palm of my hand
a tender word shouted
as in a seashell
the pattern of the labyrinth
the refrain of the wind
over a deaf ocean
from the narrow confines of memory
I kept the haunting imprint
of your breath
and your yielding face.

Je pense à la morte dans un poème
à la patience d'une statue
je suis la morte
je suis le poème dans une tombe
l'objet
rêvant de rêver l'objet
je suis la morte dans moi-même
je suis la morte dans mon poème

Narcose, p. 12

I think about the dead woman in a poem
about the patience of a statue
I am the dead woman
I am the poem in a tomb
the object
dreaming of dreaming the object
I am the dead woman in me
I am the dead woman in my poem

FOIRE

Dans une loge de cristal,
monstre rêveur de ma mémoire
sur l'étal d'une pudeur saignante
le dormeur parle:
Signal en perles flagrantes.

Narcose, p. 21

THE FAIR

In a crystal booth,
dreaming monster of my memory
displayed in bleeding modesty
the sleeper speaks:
A sign in glaring pearls.

Je veux mimer un songe absurde
faire les pas de l'oiseau qui boite
répéter un nom qui est un cri de bête
jeter en éventail une aile à la lune rongée
choisir un grain parmi les sables de vos silences
revenir sur mes pas et revenir
toujours dans la moyenne ombre
si damnée par l'aile qui me reste
je suis le signe qui vous nomme.

Narcose, p. 23

I want to live an absurd dream
mimic the gait of a crippled bird
repeat a name like the cry of a beast
throw my wing like a fan to the gnawed moon
choose a grain among the sands of your silences
and retrace my steps to keep returning
to the indifferent shadows
so cursed by my remaining wing
I am the sign that names you.

Pour fuir en vous je suis,
en vous je vous oublie.
Je couvre tous les bruits
de sorte que j'habite
la nuit de votre corps
momie qui m'enveloppe.
L'aorte est cachée.
Vous rêvez par la peau.

Narcose, p. 25

I live only to flee into you,
within you I forget you.
I smother all the sounds
so I may inhabit
the darkness of your body
the mummy that envelops me.
The-aorta is hidden.
You dream through your skin.

LE BEAU DORMEUR

Pour l'infâme un ange veille,
pour être en règle avec la nuit
pour un délit parfait, pour
le sommeil sans relief
un corps doit disparaître.

Je nage dans les tulles de mes absences
j'ai multiplié mes limites

Narcose, p. 30

120

THE PEACEFUL SLEEPER

An angel watches over the beast,
to become one with the night
for a perfect crime,
to sleep dreamlessly
a body must disappear.

I swim among the fibers of my trances
I expand my limits.

Dans le miroir   le noir s'irise,
le noir aiguise un couteau noir.
Par ce couteau qui sectionne
je suis mon tronc et deux colonnes.

Face à face dans un embu
à même la glace j'ai bu.
M'a-t-on volé, ai-je menti ?
J'ai trop rêvé, j'ai tué l'eau.

Et qui chantonne en se mirant
et se cantonne en sa beauté
n'a pas de glu pour d'autres bêtes,
il porte l'oiseau sur la tête.

Narcose, p. 35

Blackness iridescent in the mirror,
black knife honed fine by blackness.
Through this knife which slices
I am my trunk and two columns.

Face to face with a dull looking-glass
I have drunk its very image.
Have I been stolen, have I lied?
I dreamt too much, I killed the water.

And whoever sings to himself in the mirror
and confines himself in his beauty
he needs no snares for other animals
he carries the bird on his head.

De la lune givrée
l'éclat se soude en plaques
à l'immobile baroque.
Le long du mur une ombre naine
à la poursuite d'un pas désert.

Narcose, p. 39

124

The glow of the frost-covered moon
fuses into plates
like stiff baroque
Along the wall of a dwarf shadow
chases an abandoned step.

Célébration de l'absence, écume sur la nacre
embuée des coquillages ouverts - plage.
Les mots du rêve — je puis encore les prononcer,
mais déjà ils se mêlent et dans un fil s'étirent sur
le réseau placide de l'oubli.
Je m'approche d'un inconnu décidé qui ouvre le
jour.
Jadis l'on m'encourageait à ne pas ouvrir la main
sur l'oiseau captif, à "ne pas avoir peur."
Les mots du rêve sous les doigts, à l'annulaire je
sentis un coeur minuscule palpitant.

Narcose, p. 59

126

Celebration of absence, foam on dim pearlescence
of open seashells — shore.
The words of the dream — still I can pronounce them, but
    already
they spin into threads and weave into the silent fabric
of oblivion.
I approach a steadfast stranger who lets in the daylight.
In the old days they encouraged me not to open the hand
that held the captive bird, not "to be afraid."
With the words of the dream in my fist, I felt
the beating of a tiny heart at my ring finger.

Pour un exercice d'assouplissement spirituel
changer la distribution du travail des sens.
Se fier à un état de veille qui donne des éveils en
sursaut.
Par un écart extrême de soi faire un effort vers
la spécificité de chaque sensation.

Narcose, p. 67

Just to exercise the muscles of the mind
reset the pattern of the senses.
Have confidence in a vigil that gives startled
awakenings.
By creating distance from the self
make an effort to specify each sensation.

*Suivre la chemin inverse de ce qu'ingénument la
parole détruit, rentrer de plain-pied dans l'inconnu
et en accepter les termes irrévocables.
Horizon rapproché, décor pervers relié par le fil
d'une araignée immortelle. Scène du silence
comble.*

Narcose, p. 71

Follow the road that leads away from what words
naively destroy, rush headlong into the unknown
and accept its irrevocable terms.
Horizon brought closer, perverse scenery tied
together by threads of immortal spiders. Stage
of total silence.

LES OBJETS DE CHAIR SPIRITUELLE

*Il y a des sujets de rêves aux contours très nets,
faits avec des objets vrais. Ces objets sont préparés
à l'alcool et flottent dans un bocal. Trop définis
ce sont des objets de chair spirituelle. Parmi ces
objets, sous un éclairage du toutes parts, nous nous
trouvons en arrêt, privés d'ombre à la faveur de
nos prunelles factices.*

Narcose, p. 74

OBJECTS OF SPIRITUAL FLESH

Sometimes we dream of things with sharp out-
lines, made of real objects. These objects
are prepared in alcohol and float in a glass
jar. More defined they are objects of spiri-
tual flesh. Under a glaring flood of light,
we find ourselves captivated by these objects,
deprived of shadow by our empty eyes.

YVONNE CAROUTCH

YVONNE CAROUTCH:
THE MAGIC MIND

Yvonne Caroutch reflects a disruption in the perception of external sense impressions. It would be difficult, if not impossible, to isolate given "themes" in her poetry; and if one had to choose a theme it would have to be the one all-encompassing one that runs through all her poetry—that of disruption itself; and out of this disruption she tries to create a new poetic reality.

In Caroutch's works (collected in a single volume entitled **La Voie du coeur de verre,** ("The Way of the Glass Heart," 1972), we can sense a progression in the attitude of the poetic voice towards reality. In **Soifs** ("Thirst", 1954), her first book, Caroutch is content to merely record her impressions; we never know the relationship of the poetic voice to these impressions. Here, poetic vision is primarily a means to satisfy the poet's thirst for a higher, more stimulating psychic experience. In the later volumes, we see an increasingly more active involvement of the poet with the newly created world around her. After **Thirst,** the poet moves into closer proximity with her images in **Les Veilleurs endormis** ("The Sleeping Watchmen," 1955); but, as the title suggests, she is still a passive observer. In the next volume, **L'oiseleur du vide,** the title of which I have translated "Fisherman of the void" (1957), the poetic voice itself has become active, but the subject matter has become less palpable, more evanescent, approaching nothingness. Next, in **Paysages provisoires** ("Temporary Landscapes," 1965), we see an intimate, if ephemeral, union between the poetic voice and the reality around it. Finally, in **Lieux probables** ("Probable Places," 1968), the poet is even more sure of herself. She has brought the temporary into the probable, and she has strengthened the weak links of her poetic voice with the world it has created. All through this progression we see Caroutch becoming more and more agressive, more confident, more involved, more questioning of the world of images. Each stage of this progression embodies a unified attitude or vision.

Although her work may be categorized in the way I have stated, Caroutch's work also indicates a sense of structural fluidity and poetic flow. For example, none of Caroutch's individual poems is titled, only specific collections. Each poem of a given volume is only a part of a larger poem which expresses a total movement within the overall progression I have described. With the exception of the prose poems, Caroutch's poetry is virtually unpunctuated, as if commas might fragment the poem into closed sense-units which would destroy the flow from one image to the next and hinder the effects of their juxtaposition. As we move into the later volumes, however, question marks begin to occur which reflect the poet's intensified interrogation of the world of images she has created.

There is no one category from which Caroutch takes her images; animals, plants and stones of all kinds equally fuel the fires of her imagination. The various techniques which the poet uses as she goes about her transformation of reality are intimated in the following passage from one of her prose poems. She has learned to

> . . . cut a path with a subtle sword, to
> carve ever more artfully the flesh of
> destiny, with a blade ever thinner, wielded
> by a hand as deft as it is invisible.

> . . . *frayer un chemin avec un sabre subtil,*
> *de tailler de plus en plus savamment la*
> *chair de la destinée, avec une lame de*
> *plus en plus mince, maniée d'une main*
> *d'autant plus sûre qu'elle est invisible.*
> **(La Voie du coeur de verre, p. 173)**

Several distinct methods of operation are discernable as Caroutch delicately, but not timidly, cuts away at the outer surfaces of the world around her. First of all, she infuses life into inanimate objects by endowing them with human characteristics. Throughout her poetry we see images such as faces of sand, heartbeats of rain, troubled trees, drunken suns, and moving visages of rain. She intensifies the impact of matter on our perception by describing things in contradictory terms. For example, she speaks of the "flames of the snow" and the "anguish of springs asleep in stone," She evokes "frozen thoughts of lightning"; and objects are "clothed with a skin of inner being" while "blood beats in time with shadows" and "sounds are imprisoned in frozen air." Certain moods are intensified by introducing forces which negate that mood. For example, she will express silence by a chain of explosions, and will evoke night by strewing luminous dust.

Caroutch attempts to solidify airy abstractions and arrest fleeting states of mind by describing insubstantial and ephemeral realities in hard, concrete terms. Thus we have "heavy silence" and "plump darkness." Instants are capable of burning fingers, spaces can be suddenly stretched, light can be embraced. At times she tries to perpetuate movements or moments which, by their very nature, are finite. Thus she talks about "the eternal fall of silences," "timeless nights," "endless labyrinths," and "lost roads without beginning or end."

In the midst of this endless procession of visions which constantly twists and bends into new shapes before us, the word is incapable of existing alone; it must be contained in the life-giving matrix of the image. Words as they are conventionally used approximate the status of inanimate objects; they are ultimately rigid, stagnant, without life. Eventually this rigidity, this lifelessness invaded us, their users. If we do not revitalize language, words may incapacitate us:

> . . . this word that seizes us
> imprisons us in its net

> . . . *ce mot qui s'abat sur nous*
> *filet qui emprisonne*
> **(La Voie du coeur de verre, p. 85)**

In the extreme, Caroutch associates words with inertness and death:

> Words return to the dawn of rock
> like a river patiently flowing
> back to the sources of death.

> *Les mots retournent à l'aube du roc*
> *comme un fleuve qui patiemment*
> *rejoint les sources de la mort.*
> **(La Voie du coeur de verre, p. 57)**

Losing our poetic creativity, we may find ourselves speaking only "words of stone."

Caroutch turns away, then, from the mind's rational processes, and looks toward extra-rational modes of perception with which to frame her poetic vision. It is appropriate that her poems are replete with words and images which suggest the supernatural. Constantly there are references to oracles, miracles and premonitions; often objects are qualified with adjectives such as "bewitched," "secret," "lost," and "blind." Throughout Caroutch's poetry we sense a desire to enter the worlds of darkness and change, to move away from the sterile realm of reason, and to enter

> . . . the spaces dilated by dreams
> more real than any abode, the
> vehicle of all clarity.

. . . cet espace que le songe dilatait,
plus réel que toute demeure,
véhicule de toute clarté.

(La Voie du coeur de verre, p. 177)

YVONNE CAROUTCH

Yvonne Caroutch was born in Paris in 1937, of Mongolian parentage, and is married to the writer, Frederick Tristan. She has traveled extensively in Europe, Latin America, U.S.S.R., Turkey and the Near and Far East. She lived for a long time in Venice and has translated the works of Dino Campana, Montale and Ungaretti. Her own work was first recognized in 1954 when her volume of poems, **Soifs,** was hailed, along with Françoise Sagan's **Bonjour Tristesse,** as one of the two literary events of the year. In 1974 she received the Cocteau prize for **La Voie du coeur de verre,** a collected volume which contains most of the poems she has published to date. In addition to her books of poems (listed below), she has also published a play, a novella, and a number of short stories.

> **Soifs** (Nouvelles Ed. Debresse, 1954)
> **Les Veilleurs endormis** (N.E. Debresse, 1955)
> **L'Oiseleur du vide** (Structure, 1957)
> **Paysages provisoires** (Venice and New York:
> Mica, 1965)
> **Lieux probables** (La Fenêtre Ardent, 1968)
> **La Voie du coeur de verre**
> (Librairie St-Germain des Prés, 1972)

The following selections are taken from **La Voie du coeur de verre.**

Enfant du silence et de l'ombre
tu reposais dans de grands lits
d'orties sauvages et de menthe
Tu rêvais sur le fleuve immense
dévoré par un feu de lune
Tes mains répandaient dans le vent
des océans et des forêts
Où sont tes nuits ange perdu
L'aube écoute le sang trop lourd
qui bat dans les coulées d'acier
Sens-tu la peur qui entre en toi
comme un couteau dans ta poitrine
Tu marches dans notre pays
vaisseau égaré dans les bruines
Tu ne vois pas le soleil luire
comme au premier matin du monde

La Voie, p. 13

Child of silence and shadow
you were resting in large beds
of wild nettles and mint
You were dreaming on broad rivers
devoured by moonfire
Your hands expanded in the winds
of oceans and forests
Where are your nights lost angel
Dawn hears heavy blood
beating in streams of molten steel
Do you feel the fear that stabs you
like a knife in your breast
You wander through our country
like a ship lost in the mist
You no longer see the sun's glow
as you did at time's first dawn

La nuit s'ouvre comme une amande
Les soleils crèvent sur les murs
et des étoiles de chair fraîche
vont s'accrocher à nos poitrines
Les plaies s'incrustent dans le sable
L'herbe folle de nos regards
redescend parfois jusqu'au coeur
Mais nous avons dans notre sang
l'odeur des pluies dans les forêts
Nous poursuivons dans les lits froids
la chute sans fin des silences

La Voie, p. 15

142

Night opens like an almond
Suns collapse on the walls
and rosy-cheeked stars
Will cling to our breast
Wounds burrow in the sand
The weeds of our glances
Sometimes penetrate the heart
But in our blood are
Fragrances of forest rains
In cold beds we pursue
the endless fall of silences

La lumière qu'on étreint
sous le drap
Les grains de soif
qu'on jette à tous les vents
les parois du songe
qu'on déchire
à grands coups de hache
La peur stridente
qui sape les aubes furtives
Et puis nous qui recouvrons
nos détresses
de grands linges propres
Et les autres qui traversent
le lacis indéchiffré
de nos signes.

La Voie, p. 19

Light embraced
under a sheet
Grains of thirst
thrown to the wind
Walls of dream
split
with the blows of an axe
Howling fear
saps the furtive dawn
Then we who cover
our anguish
with fresh linen
And the others who cross
the undeciphered web
of our gestures.

Quand nous serons
comme deux soleils ivres
dans le silence des figues
quand la nuit moite croulera
au loin sur des villes mortes
quand nous entendrons le cri compact
des graines enfouies
sous des épaisseurs de terre
nous ferons un grand feu de menthe
pour annoncer les épousailles
de l'âme obscure des rivières
et de nos soifs multipliées

La Voie, p. 22

When we are like
two drunken suns
in the silence of figs
when moist night settles over
dead distant towns
when we hear the thick cry
of seeds buried
beneath layers of earth
we will build a great fire of mint
to announce the marriage
of the rivers' dark soul
with our endless thirst

Avec tes doigts de sel et de lumière, tu fais
lever l'aube de ma hanche. Entre la maison et le
puits surgit le regard fragile de l'espoir, comme
un éclair à l'angle du toit. Les murs s'inclinent
dans le silence, comme si la mer en nous retirait
ses assises. La solitude martèle les choses et les
revêt d'une écorce d'intimité. Les mots re-
tournent à l'aube du roc comme un fleuve qui
patiemment rejoint les sources de la mort.

La Voie, p. 57

148

With your fingers of salt and light, you raise
the dawn of my thigh. Between the house and
the well appears the fragile eye of hope, like a
bolt of lightning at the corner of the roof. The
walls bow down in the silence, as if the sea with-
in us took back its floor. Solitude batters objects
and clothes them with a skin of inner being.
Words return to the dawn of rock like a river
patiently flowing back to the sources of death.

Quelle rose des vents éclata en ces contrées
où le silence nous piquait les doigts? Les terres
se blottissaient sous l'aile de la nuit frileuse, les
poissons se figeaient dans leur auge de pierre et
les sons se prenaient dans l'air gelé ainsi que des
oiseaux. Des hommes cachant des lanternes sous
leur cape de bure surgissaient des pavés humides.
Saurons-nous jamais quelle enfance de froid nous
conduisit en cette demeure où l'obscurité nous
faisait chavirer comme un navire dans les glaces.

La Voie, p. 66

What rose of winds burst open in this land
where silence pricked our fingers? The fields
huddled under the wing of the chilly night, the
fish grew stiff in their stone bowl, and sounds
like birds became imprisoned in the frozen air.
Men hid lanterns under their rough capes wet
cobblestones appeared. Will we ever know what
frigid childhood brought us to this place where
darkness made us capsize like an icebound ship.

Les tatouages du vent sur le roc, les fausses accalmies entre deux salves de l'orage et l'attente cousue dans l'ombre des visages comme une huile douce dans la lampe. Nous cherchons le chemin du calme au noyau des fruits verts. Notre lucidité errante nous guide vers les mots de pierre. Messager de la confiance, un cheval recueille dans sa crinière des odeurs de forêts, des clameurs de ruisseaux, qu il répand longtemps après dans les étables chaudes

La Voie, p. 68

The tatoo of wind on the rock, the false calm between two bursts of thunder and the expectation sown in the shadows of faces like soft oil in the lamp. We search for the path of calm in the pits of green fruit. Our searching mind guides us to words of stone. A horse, messenger of confidence, gathers in his mane the scents of the forest, the clamor of the streams, and long after scatters them in the warm stables.

Tant de villes traversées en dormant
tant de plaines tant de lenteurs
avant de reconnaître au tranchant de l'amour
le grand corps dépecé
d'un dieu blanc sur la grève

Midi dresse ses murailles
dans l'abrupte clarté des barques
Furie solaire des tritons
des blasons des fontaines

Midi pour un visage
fermé comme une main

La Voie, p. 90

154

So many passing cities veiled by sleep
so much flatland so much languor
before the sharp edge of love
reveals the great dismembered corpse
of a white god on the beach

Midday erects its walls
in the stark light of the boats
Sun-fired fury of the newts
in the fountain blazons

Midday for a face
closed like a fist

Du sommeil la haute saison s'effrite
Nos yeux étonnés glissent dans des éboulis de lumière
La mémoire ne saute plus à la gorge comme une bête
O ce lac intérieur ce grand miroitement
Autour le silence mâche des herbes
Le chateau noir surgit dans les mosaïques célestes
L'absence et l'oubli s'ordonnent sans raison

Tropique de paille griffes cendres déesses
la folle saison bascule
--la forme de l'instant sur les eaux habitées

La voie, p. 106

In sleep the high season crumbles
Our astonished eyes slip into mountains of sunlight
No longer does memory tear at our throats like a beast
O this lake within us these myriad reflections
All around us silence chews its grass
The black castle reaches into the mosaic sky
Absence and oblivion alternate

Tropic of straw ashes claws goddesses
the mad season wavers
--the shape of the instant on living waters

Dans les grasses ténèbres tu inventes
les jeux inanimés du désir
balance du dieu qui songe
Immobile pensée de la foudre
Prolonger ce vertige
si tu ne sautes dans le fosse
pour gagner un autre rêve

La Voie, p. 168

In the heavy darkness you invent
lifeless games of desire
scales of the dreaming god
stilled thought of lightning
Prolong this anguish
if you don't plunge into the ditch
to win another dream

THERESE PLANTIER

THERESE PLANTIER:
VISIONS ALONG THE ROAD OF WATER

The constant flux of reality is an important theme for Thérèse Plantier; thus, water, ocean and fluid are important images. Not only does water suggest all that is unstable, restless and flowing, but **Chemins d'eau** ("Roads of Water"), the title of her first book, suggests that by immersing ourselves in its flow we can arrive at some destination. Plantier's roads of water almost always lead downward, into the abyss. Unlike Andrée Chedid, who is constantly looking skyward, searching out fire and light, Plantier looks ever downward and inward, turning her back on the sky, tearing away at surface realities to penetrate the mysteries of the self:

> Never so near the dream that is the void
> Never so far from congested skies

> *Jamais si proche du songe qu'est le vide*
> *Jamais si loin de l'entassement des cieux*
> **(Chemins d'eau, p. 51)**

It is here in the void of the dream that she discovers her roads of water, her "dark canal."

Closely associated with the theme of water and flux is that of the voyage (A whole section of poems in **C'est moi, Diego** ["It's me, Diego"], is entitled "Voyages"); often, references made to boats and sailing vessels can be associated either with the poet herself who takes a mental voyage into the unknown, or with the reader who takes the voyage vicariously. In the poem which begins "Beautiful tree white eternity," (p. 173) eternity is associated with the earth which nourishes the tree rather than the sky. We inscribe our confession onto the tree and thereby soothe our hunger. Although some boats—and with them the poet-voyager, the reader-passenger—are tied to the prisons of the sky, they may still hope to move, for within each boat grows the tree of eternity.

In order to join the poet on her voyages, the reader must break down certain preconceptions and must forget about the conventions which have conditioned him. "Let your memory die" she advises the reader in the opening poem of **Roads of Water.** One must not fear darkness or dreams:

> awaken shadows chase away silence
> give me night and dreams
> where the face of God never appears

éveille les ombres chasse le silence
tends-moi la nuit ses songes
où n'apparaît jamais la face de Dieu
(Chemins d'eau, p. 38)

The moment the image of God has been eliminated as the reference point for the absolute, the poet can no longer claim to know the destination of the human voyage:

Toward what shadows will we set sail
my colored one?

Vers quelles ombres partirons-nous,
ma colorée?
(Chemins d'eau, p. 38)

The fixity of a previously secure destination has been replaced in these two lines by the uncertainty of shadows. Plantier doesn't want divine help. Divinity's powers do not extend beyond a sterile bourgeois world:

come rinse the lettuce
and by this act equal the gods

viens rincer la salade
et par ce geste t'égaler aux dieux
(Chemins d'eau, p. 43)

In the midst of an ever-spreading void, God's voice speaks of nothing:

proliferating space falls prey to base diseases
here and there pustules spring forth from the void
God gossips.

en proie à d'ignobles maladies l'espace prolifère
ça et là surgissent du vide les nodosités
Dieu cancane.
(Chemins d'eau, p. 31)

The poetic world of Plantier is a universe of endless flux. There are no certainties, no constants; nothing is stable or consistent, not even the voice of the poet. Her identity, like a swift-flowing stream, constantly empties itself of the old and replenishes itself with the new. For her, life is a never-ending succession of deaths and rebirths: "I was born fifty times" *("je suis née cinquante fois")* and each new life brings with it a new identity. Like the tree, the self can be replanted in new soil, and, through the process of poetry, be regenerated at any time:

162

There is no one season to sow the body
all are good
we search under poems for the lost art

Il n'existe pas de saison pour semer le corps
toutes sont bonnes
et nous cherchons sous les poèmes la science perdue

(Chemins d'eau, p. 61)

The dream serves as a catalyst for this regenerative process:

I cannot fall asleep without becoming earth
without lifting my shroud

je ne peux m'endormir sans devenir la terre
sans rabbatre mon linceul

(Mémoires inférieurs, p. 54)

In the sense that death is the beginning of a new life, there is no reason to fear it; on the contrary, Plantier calls it "my friend death" *("mon ami la mort")*. She even fantasizes about the variety of relationships between life and death:

. . . will I come back, dead, and marry
someone living? or perhaps, newly born
to death, I'll come and haunt your table
you newly-dead to life?

. . . reviendrai-je, morte, épouser un
vivant? ou, nouvelle-née à la mort,
hanterai-je votre table, nouveaux-morts
à la vie?

(Chemins d'eau, p. 74)

"If life and death were equidistant from me," says Plantier, "I would run to meet the latter / I feel a passion for it" *("Si la vie et la mort m'étaient équidistantes / je courrais pour atteindre la seconde / j'éprouve pour elle une passion")*.

The poet's destruction of form, content and syntax, as they are conventionally conceived, must be accomplished if she is to undergo death and rebirth as transformation. She achieves this destruction in several different ways, and even speaks of it directly in her rage at middle-class thinking and in her cynicism towards its institutions:

I follow [this lie]
into your labyrinth
under the bourgeois sky

scattered with wreckage
oozing with corruption

je suis [ce mensonge]
dans tes labyrinthes
sous le ciel petit-bourgeois
foudroyé d'épaves
tartiné de corruption
                              (Mémoires inférieurs, p. 54)

Even more intense is her anger at bourgeois poets, who "know
nothing of the authentic" *("authentique on n'y comprend rien"),*
who believe that "all goes on without change" *("tout continue
pareil"),* and have a blind faith in "papo-pontifical words" *("mots
papo-pontificaux").* As a condition for rebirth, the poet must
even turn her anger upon herself:

I gnaw myself until I vomit . . .
I open my stomach
to the setting sun
without a tear without a comment

A en vomir je me grignotais . . .
je m'entr'ouvrais le ventre
au crépuscule
sans un pleur sans un commentaire.
                              (Chemins d'eau, p. 47)

Destruction is also brought to bear on the poet's own medium of
expression, on language itself. Words are not static; like the
human mind they reflect, they are constantly changing, shifting,
refocusing. Plantier breaks words out of their normal contexts,
places them into new and tension-filled juxtapositions which
reflect the processes of her own highly personal vision.

The intensity of Thérèse Plantier's poetry is created by her on-
going struggle with language itself. She is sceptical of language,
considers it a vehicle for bourgeois thinking, but, at the same
time, is tormented by a need to express herself. As one reads
through the four volumes which she has published, from **Roads
of Water** to **Jusqu'à ce que l'enfer gèle** (" 'Till Hell Freezes
Over"), one can see this struggle growing in intensity. In **Roads
of Water,** we perceive strange hallucinatory landscapes with dark
canals, black stone clearings, octopus trees, and, hovering over-
head, congested skies. These unusual juxtapositions remind one
of the techniques used by the surrealists as they lay siege to
reason and logic. But the more we follow the development of

Plantier's poetry, the more we find that her assault is on language itself rather than reason. In the introduction to her third volume, **It's me, Diego,** Plantier compares our language to an Orwellian "newspeak" wherein certain thoughts are prevented by removing from language the words which signify them:

> A good politician, George Orwell could see how, thanks to dictionaries, grammars, loudspeakers, and the servility of professors, pressure can be put on the mind to completely change it. But, being only a man, he didn't bother to ask himself if such a mental assassination hadn't already been perpetrated through the course of history.[1]

In her later volumes, Plantier uses a vocabulary which ranges from slang to scientific terminology to what could only be described as pure cacophony. One almost thinks that by using the most unusual of words in the most bizarre of contexts, Plantier is trying to clean out the hidden corners of language, and rid it of the verbiage which prevents true thought and communication. Since the poet is no longer sure whether she has anything definite to communicate through words, she no longer uses words as a reflection of meaning and therefore can only rely on the continuity of sounds. Therese Plantier must still be convinced of an internal verbal continuity even though it may lie outside the realm of immediate logical meaning. Because her poetry has moved so far into the phonetic dimension, such a passage as this one is virtually untranslatable:

> langage convulsé langage révulsé
> parturition pour bandes démagnétisées
> oh ma double hélice
> acidée
> désoxy
> ribonu
> cléique cloaquisée vingt (20) amino-acides
> nucléotides
> automate autoréplicateur ces adorables sacculines
> **(Jusqu'à ce que l'enfer gèle, p. 15)**

This clutter of words, aptly described as "convulsed language," sounds much like scientific jargon; and, as such, it is probably appropriate to call it "these adorable barnacles." It would be difficult, perhaps impossible, to find any meaning or logic to the words; and the poet's call later in the poem to "integrate them,

---

[1]C'est moi Diego, p. 9.

deary, or else they'll die" *("intégre-les chérie, ou bien elles se meurent")* must certainly be taken as ironic. What the passage does represent, though, is the process of words trying, and failing, to be words; or, to state it another way, words failing to be signs. Once the umbilical cord connecting the word with the reality it symbolizes is severed, the word ceases to be anything but a noise or a black mark on paper.

The translator has a difficult time dealing with Plantier's later work, because in poems such as the one I have just cited, the language of the poem is the subject of the poem. The strength of this poetry lies in verbal play—internal rhyme, assonance, onomatopoetic devices—which is tied to the French language.

Logic, based on cause and effect, working in fixed points in space and time, does not inform the poems of Thérèse Plantier. Rather, we are introduced to a special kind of associative movement which operates in her poetry, a "logic" which sees things simultaneously, in overlapping patterns and images, which ignores customary notions of time and space. Along with this destruction of linear logic, which assigns a given word to a given thought, Plantier also destroys the notion of a single characteristic style which assigns a particular identify to a particular writer. The only way one could characterize Plantier's style would be to say that it has no permanent character at all, that it is in a constant process of metamorphosis. At times her poetry flows softly and quietly and does not violate our rational sensibility:

> Because I breathed the first fragrance
> of summer I thought I would live a
> thousand years with you.

> *Parce que j'avais senti la première*
> *odeur de l'été j'avais cru que je*
> *vivrais mille ans auprès de toi.*
> **(Chemins d'eau, p. 65)**

At times she creates tension in the sense of a line by destroying our logical conception of space, but retains a rhythmic flow in the language itself:

> My limbs swarm with petrified reflections

> *Mes membres fourmillent de reflets pétrifiées*
> **(Mémoires inférieurs, p. 54)**

Another example:

> I touch my lips to a cup filled with night

> *J'ai porté à ma bouche la coupe emplie de nuit*
> **(Chemins d'eau, p. 74)**

But at other times this tension and rupture in sense is matched by a similar disharmony in the language itself:

> language convulsed language revulsed
> expelled foetus for demagnetized tape
> O my double helix
>
> *language convulsé language révulsé*
> *parturition pour bandes démagnétisées*
> *oh ma double hélice*
> **(Jusqu'à ce que l'enfer gèle, p. 15)**

Plantier's poetry not only "describes" the flux of life; she transcends the way words, in the logical sense, "describe" or symbolize a given reality behind them. Her poetry actually becomes identified with the flow of life. Words become part of the stream; and, because the poet is one with her words, indeed was born from her words--"language is our mommy" *("le langage est notre maman")*--the poet also becomes part of the stream. Form and content become one and the same in Thérèse Plantier.

In her poetry, words are played off against their traditionally assigned meanings. At times they are held together by sheer sound, a "logic" we can hear but not understand: *"village craqué arqué alpagué."* As these words are swept up in the swift current of her poetry, they are jostled loose from each other, each curve and bend in the stream breaks up this huge verbal logjam, and words find new positions and juxtapositions, fall into new contexts with each other and thus find new meanings. So intimately connected with this verbal flow is the poet herself that a change in language creates a change within the poet. To state it another way, the poet is able to change her own self by a change in the stream of language around her:

> In the droplets the dews the pastilles
> that flow [from poetry] I regenerate
> myself, change my essence and rise
> above nature
>
> *il en découle [de la poésie] des*
> *gouttes des pastilles des rosées où*
> *je me régénère me renature me*
> *surnature*
> **(Chemins d'eau, p. 62)**

THERESE PLANTIER

Thérèse Plantier was born in Nîmes in 1911. She began an association with the Surrealists in 1964, and contributed for a time to the journal **La Brèche.** For a while she participated in various surrealist activities, but eventually broke away from the group and returned to the South of France where she now lives in the village of Faucon. She has done several translations of contemporary British poets for **Le Pont de L'Epée.** Her published works include:

> **Chemins d'eau** (Chambelland, 1963)
> **Mémoires inférieurs** (La Corde, 1966)
> **C'est moi, Diego** (Ed. Saint-Germain-des Prés.,
> 1971)
> **Jusqu'à ce que l'enfer gêle** (Oswald, 1974)
> **La Loi du silence** (Saint-Germain-des-Prés, 1975)

il passe par la pierre le chemin d'eau
-- laisse-toi oublier --
par les pattes du chat
et par ma géographie
où les reliefs sont en dedans.

Chemins d'eau, p. 7

The road of water passes through the rock
-- let your memory die --
through the cat's paws
and through my landscape
where shapes are molded within.

Bel arbre blanc éternité
oreiller des vents
coeur des soifs
nuage enraciné
tablature confession faim calmée
qu'en toi s'enlisent les nuages
les élixirs
les sueurs
les tourments
les fins dernières
il y a un arbre dans les barques
aux pontons du ciel amarrées.

Chemins d'eau, p. 15

Beautiful tree white eternity
pillow of wind
heart of thirst
cloud with roots
empty page confession hunger soothed
may clouds
elixirs
beads of sweat
torments
and final death take root in you
in the boats moored to the prisons of the sky
there is a tree

Ta voix contient une veilleuse glacée
qui
te permet de circuler sans honte
dans la matière et dans l'eau et dans les songes
à égale distance
de la vie et de la mort
comme un petit morceau de bois
sec
comme une fente d'où le coeur aurait glissé
comme un cul-de-lampe évadé du grimoire.

Chemins d'eau, p. 30

Your voice contains a frozen lamp
that
lets you roam shamelessly
through matter through water through dreams
equidistant
from life and death
like a small piece of wood
dry
like a crack through which the heart would have slipped
like a vignette escaped from a book of black magic.

Celle qui m'attend
celle vers qui je me dirige
après bien des écarts
celle que j'ai fuie
pour mieux la rejoindre
celle dont les mains m'apaiseront
est-il dérisoire de courir les routes
afin de découvrir dans un bar
son visage derrière la pluie
des notes qui s'égouttent
d'une machine à musique?
Victime comblée
non seulement je ne fuis plus
mais encore je poursuis
c'est une réconciliation
c'est machiavélique
j'humilie la mort.

Chemins d'eau, p. 32

She waits for me
after long separations
I move toward her
I ran away from her
to join her more closely
her hands will soothe me
is it ridiculous to run the streets
to discover in a bar
her face behind a rain
of notes dripping
from a jukebox
I've had my fill
the victim is now
the pursuer
it's a reconciliation
a Machiavellian stroke
I humiliate death.

*Nuit sur la terre et amour, ambivalente nuit piquetée
de lumière où les pêcheurs militent en faveur des
poissons, où je suis ivre sans autre excuse que le goût
d'ignorer, où les pêcheurs s'unissent aux péchés
tendrement, où ce qui s'assemble se défait, pluie de
nuit sur tes lèvres et tes seins et ton ventre ronronnant,
pluie pluie sur tes bras jetés en arriére, ton épaule ma
voisine, ton cou bondissant, tes yeux à la longue
fente. Le fleuve somnole, il se repose. L'eau renonce à
tes bras, le ville s'exténue, le lierre nous étouffe. Ce
rendez-vous auquel nous ne nous rendons pas, nous
tournons autour de lui comme ces mots s'enroulent
autour de ton absence et les rues creusent plus pro-
fondes leurs rides sur mon visage. Nous circulons in
extrémis, nous accrochant à des bords de table pour
ne pas tomber, cisaillant nos chaines de lierre et ta
jupe se déchire, le temps se dechire dans l'invisible
rivière sur laquelle tu te penches..*

Chemins d'eau, p. 34

Night covers earth and love, ambivalent darkness dotted with light where fishermen fight on the side of the fish, where I am drunk with no other excuse but the sweet taste of numbness, where sinners unite tenderly with sins, where what comes together falls apart, rain of night on your lips oz your breasts your purring stomach, rain rain on your arms thrown back, your shoulder my neighbor, your neck heaving, your eyes with long slits. The river's eyes are heavy, it rests. The water renounces your arms, the tired city gasps for breath, the ivy chokes us. This meeting-place where we do not meet, we hover around it like words winding around your absence and the streets carve deeper wrinkles on my face. In the final hours we wander about clinging to the edge of the table so not to fall cutting our chains of ivy and your skirt tears, time is torn in the invisible river over which you bend.

A en vomir je me grignotais
je mâchais ma mère l'angoisse
je me détournais fatalement du devoir
j'avais recours à l'écriture
chaque fois la nuit
tirait le verrou
allumait le voyant
le judas sanglotait
transpercé jamais cicatrisé
je m'entr'ouvrais le ventre
au crépuscule
sans un pleur sans un commentaire.

Chemins d'eau, p. 47

I gnaw myself until I vomit
I chew anguish my mother
fate turns my back on duty
I turn to writing
each time night
unbolts the door
lights the beacon
the traitor sobs
wounded never healed
I open my stomach
to the setting sun
without a tear without a comment.

Afin que te cernent les fourrures et les eaux et mes rêves
afin que roulent aux égouts les cils arrachés des paupières
(pas de danger qu'on les regrette!)
afin que mugisse la brume au-dessus de ton front
marqué à mon fer
afin que vertigineux se creuse autour de toi le calice des vents
afin que malades d'incontrolable vitesse
se juxtaposent les triangles sidéraux
afin que les horloges affolées tournent si-vite qu'apparaisse
ton visage
au centre de la giration cruelle
j'intercale
des ponts silencieux
entre les cris et les vagues.

Chemins d'eau, p. 48

So that furs and waters and dreams will surround you
so that lashes torn from eyelids will flow to the sewers
(no danger of one missing them!)
so that mist will wail above your forehead
branded by my iron
so that a cup of dizzying winds will cut the air around you
so that sick with uncontrolled speed
sidereal triangles will come together
so that clocks gone mad will turn so fast that
your face
appears in the center of the cruel gyration
I place
silent bridges
between cries and waves.

Jamais si proche du songe qu'est le vide
jamais si loin de l'entassement des cieux
j'ai découvert enfin la distance réelle
le canal ténébreux
où papillonnent les voix de femmes.

Chemins d'eau, p. 51

Never so near the dream that is my void
Never so far from congested skies
I discovered at last the true distance
the murky canal
where women's voices flutter.

Rien d'étonnant comme leur certitude
aux poètes aux poétisés
que tout continue
pareil
la pluie? la pluie
l'hiver? l'hiver
ils croient avoir taillé une fois pour toutes
aux mots leurs chasubles leurs douillettes leurs mitres
ils croient aux mots papopontificaux
je suis la seule ahurie
ils se reconnaissent abondamment dans le bonheur
dans l'humain du coin dans celui qui joue au tiercé
ils se passent l'anneau violet
font courir le furet
il court il court
de plus en plus crasseux poisseux
authentique on n'y comprend rien
la pluie? saturée de pourriture
l'hiver? chaud
l'été? glacial
peu leur importe
en avant les hymnes aux saisons
les amours-cheminées-maisons
par file à droite!
si l'on meurt ce sera d'accident
et pas du sort jeté par les gitans
vive l'éducation gologolo!

Chemins d'eau, p. 59

186

Nothing's so astounding as the certainty
of the poets and the poeticized
that all goes on
without change
the rain? rain
the winter? winter
they think they've tailored a perfect-fitting costume
a stole a mitre a chasuble for words
they believe in papo-pontifical words
I'm the only one aghast
they see their reflection in happiness
in the human on the street the one who plays the horses
they make their rings around the rosey
and fill their pockets full of posey
and wallow in the filth and slime
they know nothing of the authentic
the rain? soaked with rot
the winter? hot
the summer? frozen
what could they care
march on hymns to the seasons
all you idylls-firesides-cottages
line up on the right
if one dies it's by accident
and never by a throw of gypsy dice
three cheers for education!

Il n'existe pas de saison pour semer le corps
toutes sont bonnes
et nous cherchons sous les poèmes la science perdue
le scintillement d'un rire
un oiseau un chien une vie plus fragilement écrite
un chant à deux femmes.

Chemins d'eau, p. 61

There is no one season to sow the body
all are good
we search under poems for the lost art
the scintillation of laughter
a bird a dog a life written with more delicate letters
a song for two women

LES PORTES

Elles se déploient jusqu'au ciel
ces portes je me suis enfuie
dans ma large nuit l'éternelle
sans toi
qui restes seule inquiétante
à demi-calcinée
sur ton île battue de l'épais jus
des animaux compressés
tu te dissous par ta seule puissance
tu t'enfonces par ton seul poids
au centre de la clairière en béton noir
dont s'éloignent les arbres pieuvres
chaque arbre remplacé par une porte fumigène
par un clignotant
par une maison en arc-de-cercle
ponctuée d'innombrables incinérations.

Chemins d'eau, p. 68

THE DOORS

They open themselves to the heavens
these doors I hide
in the eternal vastness of night
without you
who remain alone anguishing
half-charred
on your island beaten with thick juices
of compressed animals
undone by your own strength
sunk by your own weight
in the center of a black stone clearing
the octopus trees shy away
each one replaced by a smoking door
a blinking light
a circular house
marked by countless cremations.

Mes membres fourmillent de reflets pétrifiés
je ne peux m'endormir sans devenir la terre
sans rabattre mon linceul
comme le vent rabat aux cerisiers
leurs japons sur la tête
une fois devenue bloc
je porte en croupe les eaux
obsédantes
je ne sais jamais qui est. moi.

Mémoires inférieurs, p. 54

My limbs swarm with petrified reflections
I cannot fall asleep without becoming earth
without lifting my shroud
as the wind lifts the skirts
of cherry trees over their heads
once I am whole
I carry on my back
the haunting waters
I never know who   "I" is.

Une fleur creva
sous ta surface
se délivrant de toi
elle naquit sans que tu le saches
elle incisa
tes traits
tu crus rire
l'univers atteignit tes bornes
il ne se passa rien
qu'une chanson
la mienne
qui écuma
qui disparut.

Mémoires inférieurs, p. 67

A flower wilted
beneath your surface
freed itself from you
born unknown to you
it cut into
your features
you thought you laughed
the universe reached your boundaries
nothing happened
but a song
my   own
it bubbled up
and disappeared.

LA QUELQUE CHOSE

Ce mensonge qui te fore
je le suis à la trace
dans tes labyrinthes
sous le ciel petit-bourgeois
foudroyé d'épaves
tartiné de corruption
entre les cieux périodiques
publies chaque matin
ton idéal donne de la bande
il s'est crevé sur quelque mine
il est temps de retourner au village
où la pluie dissout le fer
où le rouge éteint le blanc
afin d'y apprendre qu'on mentait
et de ne plus croire jamais
qu'aux hiboux protecteurs des pêches
à la tête humaine fruit des arbres
à nos empreintes pour y manger.

Mémoires inférieurs, p. 67

SOMETHING

This lie that penetrates you
I follow its tracks
into your labyrinth
under bourgeois skies
scattered with wreckage
oozing with corruption
between the daily heavens
issued each morning
your ideal is listing
a mine has pierced its hull
it's time to go back to the village
where rain dissolves the steel
and red extinguishes white
there we'll learn they've lied
we'll learn to believe no one
but the owls that protect the peaches
human heads fruit to be eaten
from the trees that bear our stamp.

SI PROCHES

sous tes paupières un instant rebroussées
germa une coccocinelle
dont l'orange chemina
sagement
de ta joue à ma joue
je le notai sur cette feuille

C'est moi, Diego, p. 62

SO CLOSE

under your eyelids turned up for an instant
grew a ladybug
its orange hue
softly flowed
from your cheek to mine
I wrote it on this page

Jamais ville ne fut plus absente
plus lointaine plus incertaine
sur ses reflets tortillés
on pourrait y marcher à plat en tous sens
nager à travers ses trottoirs
taper du talon sur les eaux des carénages
se ligoter avec les colliers
des ampoules à la queue leu leu
par le travers du ciel sablonneux
rien ni personne n'y circule
surtout pas les voitures
aveugles comme des taupes
conduites souterrainement
au fond des égouts
qu'une pellicule humaine dissimule.

C'est moi, Diego, p. 110

200

Never a city more absent
more distant more uncertain
on its foundations its fluids
its twisted reflections
there one could walk flat in all directions
swim across its sidewalks
strike the waters of shipyards
chain oneself with a necklace
of lightbulbs
against the sand-filled sky
there no motion of persons or things
and above all no cars
blind as moles
they are driven underground
in the depths of sewers
concealed by a human film.

Vêtue ornée de très grandes terreurs
j'erre sous la peau nacrée de la terre
cherchant dans l'une des quatre maisons du monde
le vase-conque où reposent mes viscères
ivrogne itinérant
clocharde infra-terrestre
je ne voudrais plus voir mais discerner
à travers les blêmes girations
au fond du désordonné
parmi les racines enchevêtrées aux abîmes
les tentacules germées dans ce vase-écubier
mes yeux empennés se plantent
dans les épouvantables cibles
derrière devant dessus dessous
je tourne de plus en plus ronde
n'éprouvant aucune honte
projectile astucieux
je transperce en son centre en sa géométrie
en sa reserve mathématique
en son vol
l'alphabet des cendres universelles
entassées sur l'espoir
plue dans toutes ses fissures
je le ronge patiemment
puisque c'est le coeur où se figent

Adorned in garments of terror
I roam under the earth's nacreous skin
seeking in the world's four houses
the conch-shaped vase where lie my viscera
wandering drunkard
infra-terrestrial beggar
I no longer want to see but discern
through the pale gyrations
at the heart of chaos
among the vines entangled in the chasms
the tentacles rooted in the bottomless vase
my arrow glances
strike the terrifying targets
that surround me
faster and faster I spin
feeling not an ounce of shame
a cunning projectile
I explode in its center in its geometry
in its mathematical potential
in its flight
the alphabet of universal ashes
heaped upon hope
I rain down upon its fissures
I gnaw it patiently
for at its core

d'un seul coup
les cristaux de l'invisible
et les dernières frontières
bâillonnées de lambeaux d'âme
mais tenace
je fuis l'ailleurs
là où depuis longtemps s'irisent les dégradations
s'étirent en strates les péninsules
sale machinerie
j'observe
emmurée dans l'infini crayeux
le cancer de la matière grignoter le temps
avec ses petites mâchoires ses lèvres ses suçoirs
devenir pieuvre
étoile
s'étirer le long du vase
dont la profonde forme
enfonce ses doigts dans la nuit et les vaisseaux.

C'est moi, Diego, pp. 134-35.

in a single fusion
unite the crystals of the unseen
with last frontiers
gagged with shreds of soul
but I can't let go
I flee the foreign places
where ageless stratified colors glow
and timeless peninsulas stick out in layers
all a foul deception
walled up in an infinity of chalk
I watch
the cancer of matter nibble at time
with its jaws its lips its suckers
become an octopus
a star
envelop the vase
whose penetrating form
digs its fingers into night and the vessels.

BIBLIOGRAPHY

Selected Critical Works

Alyn, Marc. **La Nouvelle poésie française.** Les Hautes Plaines de Manes: Robert Morel, 1968.

Bosquet, Alain. **Verbe et Vertige: Situations de la Poésie.** Paris: Hachette, 1961.

Friedrich, Hugo. **The Structure of Modern Poetry.** Evanston: Northwestern, 1974.

Isaacs, J. **The Background of Modern Poetry.** New York: Dutton, 1952.

Raymond, Marcel. **From Baudelaire to Surrealism.** London: Methuen, 1970.

Anthologies of Contemporary French Poetry

Aspel, Alexander and Donald Justice, eds. **Contemporary French Poetry.** Ann Arbor: University of Michigan Press, 1965. Bilingual.

Aspinwall, Dorothy Brown, ed. **French Poems in English Verse.** Metuchen, N.J.: The Scarecrow Press, 1973. Bilingual.

Burnshaw, Stanley, ed. **The Poem Itself,** New York: Schocken, 1967.

Coon, Stephen, ed. **The Ear of the Bull.** Providence: Bonewhistle Press, 1974. Bilingual.

Fowlie, Wallace, ed. **Mid-Century French Poets.** New York: Twayne, 1955. Bilingual.

Gascoyne, David, ed. **Collected Verse Translations.** London: Oxford, 1970.

Gavronsky, Serge, ed. **Poems and Texts.** New York: October House, 1969.

Marissel, André, ed. **Poètes vivants.** Paris: Millas-Martin, 1969.

Martin, Graham Dunstan, ed. **Anthology of Contemporary French Poetry.** Austin: University of Texas Press, 1971. Bilingual.

Mowrer, Paul Scott, ed. **A Choice of French Poems.** Francestown, N.H.: Golden Quill Press, 1969.

Modern Poetry in Translation. No. 41 (1970).

Mundus Artium. Vol. 7, no. 1 (1974). Bilingual.

Rexroth, Kenneth, ed. **100 Poems from the French.** Cambridge: Pym-Randall, 1972.

Shapiro, Norman, ed. **Négritude.** New York: October House, 1970. Bilingual.

Taylor, Simon Watson and Edward Lucie-Smith, eds. **French Poetry Today.** New York: Schocken Books, 1971. Bilingual.

Anthologies of Contemporary French Women Poets

Mundus Artium. Vol. 7, no. 2. (1974). Bilingual.

Poésie I. Vol. 6, (1969), Vols. 39/40 (1975).

Moulin, Jeanine. Huit siecles de poésie féminine. Paris: Seghers, 1975.

Surveys of Contemporary French Poetry

Brindeau, Serge, ed. La Poésie contemporaine de langue francaise depuis 1945. Paris: Ed, St.-Germain-des-Prés, 1973.

De Boisdeffre, Pierre. Les Poètes français d'aujourd'hui. Paris: Presses Universitaires de France, 1973.

Le Magazine littéraire, Vol. 47.

Books and Articles on Poetry Translation

Arrowsmith, W., and R. Shattuck, eds. The Craft and Context of Translation. Austin: University of Texas Press, 1961.

Brower, Reuben, ed. On Translation. Cambridge: Harvard University Press, 1959.

Carne-Ross, D.S. "Translation: Some Myths for its Making." Delos. No. 1, p. 205-15.

Cary, Edmond. "Traduction et Poésie." Babel, Vol. 3, No. 1, p. 11-32.

Holmes, James S. "Forms of Verse Translation and the Translation of Verse Form." Babel, Vol. 15, No. 4, p. 195-201.

Nims, John Frederick. "Poetry: Lost in Translation." Delos, Vol. 5, pp. 108-126.

Raffel, Burton. "How to Read a Translation: Poetry." Books Abroad, Vol. 41, pp. 279-85.

Translation 73. Vol. 1, (1973).

Translation 74. Vol. 1, (1974).

Will, Frederic. The Knife in the Stone. The Hague: Mouton, 1973.

PERIVALE TRANSLATIONS

No. 1 THE ROMAN SONNETS OF GIUSEPPE GIOACCHINO
BELLI, translated by Harold Norse with his introduction,
notes, and designed cover after a Pinelli print. Preface by
William Carlos Williams.
54 pages. $3.00 paper.
ISBN 0-912288-06-X LC No. 73-79284

"This modified version . . . should be warmly received by
the American reading public." **(Choice)**

No. 2 YIDDISH SAYINGS MAMA NEVER TAUGHT YOU:
humor and folklore. Translated by G. Weltman and M.S.
Zuckerman from the 1908 work by Ignaz Bernstein with
introduction by the translators and commentary by
translators and original compiler.

Yiddish, YIVO transliteration, and English version.
99 pages. Designed cover. $3.95 paper.
ISBN 0-912288-04-3 LC No. 79282

"This book will hold its own on your shelf of Yiddish
folklore." **(Tzaddikim Review)**

"A charming addition to Yiddish folklore." (I.B. Singer)

". . . juicy, savoury, spicy." (Henry Miller)

No. 3 EPIGRAMS FROM MARTIAL, translated by Richard
O'Connell with an introduction by the translator and a
preface by Guy Daniels.
59 pages. $3.75 paper.
ISBN 0-912288-07-8 LC No. 76-3066

"O'Connell is probably the finest epigrammatist in
America today." **(Littack - England)**

"These superb translations capture the essence of the
satiric Martial." **(The Classical Review)**

OTHER PERIVALE TITLES

POETS WEST, an anthology of contemporary poems
from the Western states edited and introduced by
Lawrence P. Spingarn.
162 pages. Designed cover. $5.50 paper.
ISBN 0-912288-05-1 LC No. 73-79233

". . . an excellent new anthology . . ." **(San Francisco
Chronicle)**

MADAME BIDET & OTHER FIXTURES, poems by Lawrence P. Spingarn. 29 pages. Designed cover. $2.50 paper. 3rd printing. ISBN 0-912288-00-0.

"Spingarn has a quiet voice that demands attention because of his authentic feelings combined with sophisticated juxtaposition" **(Choice)**

FREEWAY PROBLEMS & OTHERS, poems by Lawrence P. Spingarn. 40 pages. Cover by Wayne LaCom. ISBN 0-912288-02-7. $2.00 paper. ISBN 0-912288-01-9. $4.00 cloth.

"Spingarn writes a piquant, perceptive verse that has won him a growing, eclectic following . . ." **(Los Angeles Herald-Examiner)**

THE BLUE DOOR & OTHER STORIES, by Lawrence P. Spingarn (to appear).

THE JEWISH MOTHER GOOSE, humor by Harry Squires, with his introduction and a foreword by George Jessel. 64 pages. Designed cover. $3.95 paper. ISBN 0-912288-09-4. LC No. 76-55685

". . . read and enjoy Mr. Squires' **The Jewish Mother Goose** and you will be as thankful to this delightfully humorous writer as I am." (George Jessel)